A Mirroring Discovery...
with Angel Visitation!

Gloria Messenger

Copyright © 2011 Gloria Messenger

All rights reserved. No part of this book may be used or reproduced by
any means, graphic, electronic, or mechanical, including photocopying,
recording, taping or by any information storage retrieval system
without the written permission of the author except in the case
of brief quotations embodied in critical articles and reviews.

ISBN: 978-1-4525-4009-2 (sc)
ISBN: 978-1-4525-4010-8 (e)
ISBN: 978-1-4525-4008-5 (hc)
Library of Congress Control Number: 2011918143

Balboa Press books may be ordered through booksellers or by contacting:

Balboa Press
A Division of Hay House
1663 Liberty Drive
Bloomington, IN 47403
www.balboapress.com
1-(877) 407-4847

Because of the dynamic nature of the Internet, any web addresses or
links contained in this book may have changed since publication and may
no longer be valid. The views expressed in this work are solely those
of the author and do not necessarily reflect the views of the publisher,
and the publisher hereby disclaims any responsibility for them.

The author of this book does not dispense medical advice or prescribe the use
of any technique as a form of treatment for physical, emotional, or medical
problems without the advice of a physician, either directly or indirectly. The
intent of the author is only to offer information of a general nature to help
you in your quest for emotional and spiritual well-being. In the event you use
any of the information in this book for yourself, which is your constitutional
right, the author and the publisher assume no responsibility for your actions.

Printed in the United States of America

Balboa Press rev. date: 10/28/2011

To those who desire a glimpse of understanding of this earthly spiritual journey we have taken on!

A Loving Angel Hug of Thank You ... to

My husband, William—I teasingly blame you for what happened to me, but the truth is I am so grateful for your unaware part, or as you put it—*in spite of me*—involvement in the discovery of this awesome Angel connection.

Sharon—a daughter so special, as your wonderfully loving gifts and quiet wisdom are obvious. Alvin—your timely comic antics are so refreshingly enjoyable, looking forward to the next one. Gary—my son, sharing your uniquely original humour keeps me laughing, and that is contagious. Kimberly—your infectious giggle, and storytelling warms my heart.

Scott, Nancy, Catherine—and Laura, Ken, Jim—a family embrace so priceless an irreplaceable gift. And, I believe that *the women still rule* with Pictionary.

Our precious grandchildren—Alyssa, Chelsey, Sarah, Leah, Braydon, Callum, Keagan, Maxwell, and Charlie. Every one of you is so full of opportunity and promise for the future. So reach—*to infinity and beyond!*

My sisters and brothers—I am blessed with three sisters and two brothers (Marilyn, Linda, Darlene, Dwight, Kevin). Your part in cherishing the years of memories and diligently keeping our family ties strong would definitely make Mom proud. Sisters-in-law and brothers-in-law, nieces and nephews, so glad you chose to join our unique family with all its gatherings and interaction. I will always treasure our *Vanity Fair* photo shoot. Our blended family and extended family would not be complete without my sister-in-law Patricia. Sharing of your mother's unique sayings will always crack me up and the loving welcome you enthusiastically display also mimics your mission to share.

Lorraine Willett— a long-time friendship I treasure. Future travel and fun adventures are surely slotted in both of our itineraries. Your natural ability to celebrate who you truly are is bodacious. Carolyn Shannon—I am blessed to find a soul sister like you. As we journey forward together, just want to yell—*You Go WOW Gal!* Terri McCallum—when we met, we shared a passion for real estate that turned into a lasting friendship. Cheers to us as we each take on our futures itineraries of pre-designed miracles!

I am blessed with many spirited friends like Greeba-Ann Birch, Ginny Schumacher, Lee Royer, Ginette Hunter, and Sue London, to name only a few. Your juncture in my life is surely divinely guided. We must remember to keep our Ever-Ready motivational batteries fully charged for the road ahead. I am forever grateful to enjoy so many beautiful souls continuously interacting in my itinerary of life here. There is priceless treasure in each and every one of these friendship.

Amazing insight awaits us within this book. Get ready—buckle up—here we go!

Illustrations

❖ **Four Identical Sister Dresses:**
A memory sketch of the four identical dresses sewn by our mother for each of her four daughters during our growing years. These dresses were passed down as each girl moved into the next dress size. This sketch was designed by my sister and award winning artist Linda *(Messenger)* Callander as one of her surprises during our 2002 sisters' get-together.

❖ **Angel Vision colouring:**
This portrait colouring of the Angel vision she saw at age two and half was created when Alyssa was four years of age. The original crayon drawing by my granddaughter, of the Angel she saw, displays a rainbow of colours as it twirls around and around. *(black and white print for this book)*

❖ **Book cover design:**
The image on the cover of this book was purchased for use from Photolibrary Group, Inc. of New York, NY, USA. This image is reflective of a divinely guided story shared within this book. *(Read story in - Chapter thirteen - Emotional Awe.)*

❖ **Emotional Pulse:**
This sketch was received via The Angels of The Light. I saw this sketch visually displayed within my mind as it was being placed on paper. The Angel's wing is shown taking a pulse to indicate the raise or elevation of our pulse in an emotional experience of choices.

Contents

Illustrations vii
Introduction.. xv
Preface xvii
Chapter 1—The Early Years................................. 1
Chapter 2—Becoming Aware of Choices 11
Chapter 3—Disillusionment—Mixed Emotions.......... 17
Chapter 4—Spreading My Wings! 23
Chapter 5—Grandchildren and Other Miracles 31
Chapter 6—A Happiness High 39
Chapter 7—Angel Visitation................................. 45
Chapter 8—Name Meaning and Mission Confirmation 53
   Overview Mission—Mission/Purpose—Focus Requirement—Intended Directive—Desired Support
Chapter 9—Granddaughter's Angel Vision! 63
Chapter 10—My Story Takes Flight....................... 67
   Overview Missions—Emotional Pulse—Balance/Off-Balance
Chapter 11—Linking with Our Angels..................... 75
Chapter 12—Insight from the Heavens 85
   Energy—Light—Colour
   Section 1: What are Angels?.......................... 85
   Section 2: Questions—Questions—Questions: 90
   Section 3: Levels of Growth:..........................113
   Section 4: The ALL Love: 120

Expression of Love—Me and My Shadow

Section 5—Abundant Choices: 134
- A) Visual Thought of The ALL and Angel Connection: 136
- B) Gaining the Big Picture of our Soul Journey Preparations: 137
- C) A Secondary Path—Shadow Path: 137
- D) The Choice of Gifts: 140
- E) Multiple and Group Choices: 142
- F) Why do you Choose Illness? 145
- G) The Work is Never Done until it is Done: .. 146
- H) Seeking Clarity—to Lift the Veil of Forgetfulness: 148
- I) Further Assistance!—Twelve Areas of Further Assistance from the Source of ALL: 150
  - a. Choice of Character—Self-Preservation Option and Self-Motivation Focus. 150
  - b. Connecting with Other Souls: 153
  - c. Side Ventures: 154
  - d. A Swing Exchange/Venture: 155
  - e. Choice of Full Action: 157
  - f. Choice of Withdrawal Action: 158
  - g. Time Out Call Choice to Reincarnation: 159
  - h. Other Options of Soul Growth: 160
  - i. A Glimpse into the Teaching of the Need for Soul Growth: 160
  - j. Retention of Your Souls' Growth: 163
  - k. Trust within Self: 167
  - l. Abundant Blessings: 169
- J) Further Questions: 172
- K) Levels of Intention: 177
  - a. Intention Level to Hold Placement: 180
  - b. Level of Lightness and Joy: 181
- L) The Carriage of Completion: 183

M) Colours of Lightness and Joy: 185
N) Blending of Energies within Colours: 185
O) Preparation to Gain Clarity: 188
P) Sense of Self-Knowing: 189
Q) Observer—Twin Experience: 189
R) A Positive Self-Absorption: 192
S) Signs of Guided Wisdom: 193
T) What is pulling Your Carriage? 197
U) Journey of Engagement of ALL Love: 200
V) Our Soul Family on Earth: 204
W) Intersection of Distraction: 209
X) Intersection of Attraction: 211
Y) An Expression of Passion: 212
Z) An Area of Humour: 215

Section 6: The Expression of Emotions: 217
    a. Take Your Emotional Pulse: 218
    b. Lifting Self into Observation of The
       ALL Unconditional Love: 221

Section 7: Answers from The Angels—
       Our Mission Companions: 225

Section 8: Selection of Passion:
       (Joy—Peace—Trust): 228

Section 9: Time as Compared to No-Time: 230

Section 10: Incarnation—A Bigger Picture: 232

Section 11: A Journey of Expression: 235

Section 12: Gifted Talents, Traits, and Abilities: ..237
    a. Soul Growth Application: 241
    b. An Enabling Trait Scenario: 242
    c. Expression of Talents: 247
    d. Layering Adventure (Adoption): 248

Section 13: Angel Alerts: 249
    a. Lightness of Path: 251

    b. Steps to Completion: 252
    c. No Judgment of The ALL Source: 254
    d. Debriefing Scenario: 256

Chapter 13—Who's Cookie Are You? 263
    Vision of Confirmation—Recognition Exercise—Five-Part Harmony —Emotional Awe —My Soul Song—Words from the ALL Source.

Conclusion 297

Glossary 299

Endorsements 301

Your journey there is a journey of discovery.

**The reflection of a mirror does assist—
in elevation to Soul growth …
The Angels of The Light.**

Introduction

This book is offered to engage an open thought to the concept of pre-determining our life path with the ever-present intention of soul growth. It is my desire as a messenger—to inspire a discovery of the somewhat hidden clues placed within our life journey.

    This book is presented in a narrative conversation between my Soul voice, my conscious Mind voice, and the heavenly voice of The ALL and The Angels of The Light. It is a sharing of wisdom from the heavens to offer a glimpse of my predesigned itinerary events plus truly amazing insight. During meditation sessions I receive automatic writings via The All *(God/Creator)* and/or The Angels of The Light. These automatic writings are quoted throughout this book presented with hyphenated (—) punctuation. This hyphen is my attempt to mimic the continuous flow of these writings.

Identifying the speaker:

- My Soul Voice—is a representation of my inner intuitive thoughts lifted during these conversations and is received in channelled automatic writings.

- My Mind Voice—is a representation of the thoughts in my Mind during these conversations. These writings are both channelled and also conscious awareness. *My questions and wonderings are shown in italics.*

- **The Angels of The Light**—these writings are channelled automatic writings presented in **a**

bold font and direct quotes received from **The Angels of The Light / The ALL.**

➢ **Angel glimpse of my pre-selected Itinerary Events**—are shown in **bold font** and received from **The Angels of The Light** via automatic writings.

Note: The Angels of The Light often use a seemingly *Old English dialect* in the automatic writings that I receive. Further inquiry on why they choose to give messages using this dialect produced the following answer:

Response: **This chosen dialect offers us the ability to reach out in a way that leaves the reader with the expanding thought to digest and receive the Ahah! of understanding—in this dialect there is the gain of an impact of understanding to open the mind into grasping the message—the reader must slow to gain and glean the message and thereby reflect on the thought—if one's familiar with a slower pace—then the messages are clearer—if one's of a faster pace—the message does whiz by—we offer this example—*the reflection is within the reflection and of the reflection*—or—*a message is within and of the message.***

(For a further example: reflect on the idiom—**when we can't see the forest for the trees**—this expression entertains the thought that when a broader view is taken we can go beyond what is right in front of us, where a wondrous adventure could be displayed**.)**

Preface

This book was channelled or received via automatic writings from The Angels of The Light within a thirty-three day span. I consider this an amazing feat for my first published book.

As The Angels continuously entertain me, they presented the last chapter first when starting this book. You will note that when their insightful information appears to overwhelm comprehension, they will insert lightness with the use of their enjoyable humour.

This word *itinerary* is used by The Angels of The Light within this book to present and identify the pre-planning undertaken by the Soul team prior to birth here on earth. This itinerary event is offered as an insightful glimpse to our journey and life adventure chosen here.

> ➢ Funk & Wagnall's Dictionary offers this meaning of the word itinerary: a detailed account or record of a journey.

**We are of the ALL love—
and do embrace you—
in this emotionally engaging lift—
to assist your clarity of path—
... The Angels of The Light.**

Chapter One:

The Early Years

This dialogue of interaction begins as my Soul voice relates to the glimpse of the first itinerary entry. This is a glimpse of my predesigned Soul growth journey as given by The Angels of The Light. These Angels of The Light, who are self-described as the vibrations of the Source of ALL, begin to show my Mind glimpses of these itinerary events. Come along for this amazing adventure of Insight on the Wings of The Angels of The Light!

First Event: Itinerary glimpse given by The Angels of The Light:

> Birth Record:
>
> **Weight: 7 lbs. 13 ½ ounces**
> **Length: 20 inches**
>
> **Hair: black   Eyes: blue**
>
> **Comments: Healthy baby girl.**
> **First Name: Gloria**
> **Surname: Messenger**

The Early Years

My Soul begins to communicate:
Thanks for this reminder, Angels. Mmmm—good—okay ... my first two clues are in place! Begin with baby steps as instructed. Yes, I realize the need for this slow pace; hope to find comfort in such a small form. Here we go! Do I need to buckle up?

My Mind begins to recognize the Soul's presence:
Can you hear me now? *My Soul speaks out as it begins this life journey in the small body of Gloria Messenger. Its ever-present position is secured as its journey of life begins to unfold. This Soul growth comes from the daily gain of understanding by my Mind as it observes life choices and their consequences.* Is someone inside me talking?

My Mind hears:
My Mind now identifies this voice of knowledge as the designer of its life itinerary. As the Soul offers recognition of each event presented to the Mind; open conversation results. A third party enters these conversations in Angel voices of guidance as the itinerary events are presented and a continuous three-way dialogue of insight results. This journey is navigated with observation to the fallout or effect that personal choices have on my Soul and other Souls in my family group. So, this places me, the Mind, into self-discovery? This is all so very interesting, acknowledges the Mind. Time to wake up now! We have a lot to communicate on this adventure with the assistance of our Angels, the Soul's words are heard. There is a bigger plan selected for my life, my Mind repeats. Cool! I just love adventures!

My Soul expresses:
Oh … whew … blah … burp whahhhh …waaah … waah … wah!—am I hungry?—am I tired?—do I really know? Oops think I soiled myself—clean up please—whahhhh waah wah! This confinement of a baby's body and inability to communicate is becoming very trying on my nerves … Oh! … I have nerves? Wow, new things every day! I trust this body will grow quickly to allow my energy as a Soul to expand as I take on this life mission. Focus now, must expand this Mind's attention span. Now let's get things moving forward. What was my next pre-designed entry?

Entry: Itinerary glimpse from The Angels of The Light:
You have an older sister and, within the next two years, you will also share your life with two more sisters—then eight and thirteen years later - two brothers will complete your siblings.

My Soul enjoys:
Good, all seems to be going according to my plan and now the bonding begins. It is fun at this stage when there is still some Soul recognition between my siblings. Too bad this Mind must agree to forget our itinerary entries as the body grows into our youth, teen, and adult years. But there would be no need for this discovery of soul growth, if all was remembered before we began the adventure.

Entry: Itinerary glimpse from The Angels of The Light:
Two sisters join your family—four little girls now—your mother has her hands full—

The Early Years

however—she will celebrate each of her four daughters with birthday parties inclusive of cakes—gifts—decorations—photos and much family fun memories.

My Soul expresses:
Playing with my sisters is interesting. To play and expand the imagination of the Minds is necessary. I am enjoying these fun days with our creative games, innocent wild adventures. This too is soul growth. Wonder when our individual Minds' will develop their voices? Looking forward to communicating with them!

My Soul expands:
The playing, getting along, leading, following, engaging, and listening are the baby steps. I am aware of the need for this practise to make choices in life, yes. Up to the age of six, my Mind will recall our mission choice and then begin to forget what the itinerary of each life adventure includes. Then the real work begins for us Souls, as we begin to prompt and lead our Minds with an inner dialogue.

Entry: Itinerary glimpse from The Angels of The Light:
You will begin an education process— reading—writing—arithmetic—it is called the three R's—*(spell check someone)* you will be tested on how well you retain these teachings— you will be taught about God— many gaps of information will compel you to ask questions for clarity— the answers will be incomplete and you will begin to rely on your inner knowing— you will be rich with

choices—as you are gifted this free will of thought choice—you will enjoy the fun of siblings as you grow—however you will feel somewhat alone and often different in your approach to life—this is a result of your Soul voice offering you a glimpse of your chosen mission as it is uniquely yours—it differs from others in the approach or application used to assist self and other souls on their own unique journey.

My Soul confirms:
Oh yeah, as a Soul this journey isn't just a walk in the park—there is work to be done!

Entry: Itinerary glimpse from The Angels of The Light:
Your mother will display her creative abilities to make ends meet—you will observe and absorb these abilities for your future needs—she will dress her four little daughters in *love-dresses* that she will sew—these dresses will have red hearts floating all over a white background—these dresses will become part of your memory as they will be passed down through the girls until you all grow out of them—she will present the four daughters as if you were her quadruplets—the same dresses and hairstyle will display a sister family unit.

The Early Years

Sisters' Dresses

This sketch of memory by my sister Linda *(Messenger)* Callander, was transferred onto T-shirts of the four sisters. We proudly wear and cherish this look-alike-sisters childhood memory as we celebrate over twenty years of our sister get-together retreats.

My Soul recalls:
Cherishing our good memories and releasing our hurtful ones. Oh, yes, I remember now how that works to give me a self-confident swagger in life. Quickly jump the puddles of emotional hurts so they do not linger and take over my Mind's thoughts. Learn the lesson and release the hurts to dissolve in the universe—off you go! *Accentuate the positive—Eliminate the negative—Say no to Mr.*

In-Between! Those are the lyrics to an old song. Am I truly hearing these words sung in my Mind?

Entry: Itinerary glimpse from The Angels of The Light:
Your Mother will continue to be the biggest influence in your life—she will enroll you in tap dance—Brownies—and encourage harmonizing song performances with your three sisters at school concerts.

My Mind inquires:
Is there still time to play as we take on this adventure, Soul? I do so enjoy playing with not a care in the world.

My Soul answers:
Hello, Mind, I have been waiting to hear from you! Yes, this ability to play will serve us well into the future. Happy to see you are consciously awake now. Let us keep this communication line open, as it will also serve us well.

Entry: Itinerary glimpse from The Angels of The Light:
Your older sister will become influential to you as she discovers her gift of divine- *(God/The ALL)* **musical talent—your mother purchases a second-hand upright piano—your sister sits down and begins to play without having any lessons—to the marvel of your family— remembering this gift on a subconscious level, her fingers fly over the ivory and ebony keys—you will quickly realize that you have not received this gift to play piano—as she**

patiently explains the keys to press for a duet.

My Mind reluctantly accepts:
Okay, I am sleepy. Alright then, as my older sister she can stay up for a while longer and play music with the adults at our family house parties. Off to bed I go. Cannot wait to recognize my God-given talents! Wonder what they will be?

Entry: Itinerary glimpse from The Angels of The Light:
When you reach eight years young, your family expands to receive another sibling—a little baby brother—this is a unique experience to keep your inner child alive and you play with him like a real live doll—your mother will now have four in-home babysitters.

My Soul comments:
Is it getting crowded in here or is it just the cramped space of this two-bedroom bungalow? *Snug as bugs in a rug—whew!* Mom—Dad—do you think it is time to move?

Entry: Itinerary glimpse from The Angels of The Light:
Your family moves to a two-story - four-bedroom home to the other side of your neighbourhood—meeting new friends is exciting to you and the adventure of discovering your little world continues.

My Mind reacts:
Oh, I was looking forward to sharing my bedroom with only one other sister? Boarders? What are they? It is a new concept to me to have strangers

pay to rent a bedroom in our home. Mom says *it helps make ends meet.* Well, these digs are more spacious than the last ones. Oh, and there are secret hidey-holes to explore in the eves. We still have our outdoor surroundings yet to discover. With so many exciting new adventures, maybe there will be some more growth for you, Soul. What do you say?

My Soul responds:
You have barely begun with this adventure of life—there is so much more growth to experience. This is just a little glimpse of insight here from our Angel companions on this journey.

**As it is to the ALL love—
we do lift to your attention.**

**It is to this vision of observing self—
within and of this ALL love—
that propels your choices of best—
... The Angels of The Light.**

Chapter Two:
Becoming Aware of Choices

Entry: Itinerary glimpse from The Angels of The Light:
You are surprised to learn a new baby brother will soon join your family—you are now thirteen years young—high school with all its soul-growth potential is in your sights.

My Mind comments to itself:
This little brother is cute, but I cannot spend all my spare time babysitting. I need to venture out more. It's intriguing how some friends choose to focus their attention on other things. What could be more important than hanging out together in our gang? Is there soul growth somewhere out there that I could be missing?

Entry: Itinerary glimpse from The Angels of The Light:
As you share in this family life—you will grow into your teenage years and become intrigued with boys your age—your older sister will be a wealth of knowledge and influence to you—she will set up double dates with her and boys—you are not impressed with the boys she picks for you.

My Mind wonders:

Am I just the convenient cover of taking a younger sister along, so our mom thinks my older sister will less likely get into any trouble? I think I am catching on to this. However, I do like the privilege of sitting in on her secret girlfriend pow-wow gatherings. What was it that I am not to tell Mom? *Oh yeah, she never took a puff, Mom!* So many younger sister rules I must remember. Will I do the same to my younger sisters?

Oh, and babysitting other peoples' kids! Not too keen on this, but the money is good. It does cramp my social life though. Do really enjoy the school dances and hanging out with friends.

My Soul offers:

These years are the formative years of moving into early awareness of self, my Mind friend. These teen discovery years can offer a glimpse of the Soul, to alert and guide you here. We have many adventures ahead—of self-discovery!

Entry: Itinerary glimpse from The Angels of The Light:

In grade ten— you think you have met Mr. Right—you date him exclusively for two years—he is a sports jock and introduces you to basketball and a full social calendar with intimacy plus an opportunity to escape the verbal fighting at home—your parents will soon separate and end their marriage.

My Mind queries:

Was this intimacy I craved a result of the distress of my home life? Am I, at the age of eighteen, a young adult with my full life ahead of me, able to make wise choices?

Entry: Itinerary glimpse from The Angels of The Light:
You begin to visualize going out on your own right after school ends—getting married and having a happy family—your doodle on your school books in your best penmanship—Mrs. _____.

My Mind wonders:
Do I really get what I ask for? Could visualization be a powerful tool that I want to learn to access in a manifesting way? I sense big changes coming. What happens next in my itinerary?

Entry: Itinerary glimpse from The Angels of The Light:
You choose to marry your high school sweetheart and begin a life together—now with a new precious baby girl in tow— you move to another city that is an hour away from your hometown—many soul growth experiences wait—you focus upon using your creative talents to cook—bake—clean—sew— and put love and comfort into your home.

My Mind justifies:
Yes, this is certainly a wise choice. I have left the dysfunction of my parents' home life and am focusing on my new life with my husband and new baby. *What other choices were available to me? A career? Travel? More life experiences, more wisdom?* I would not choose to give up the love and joy that I now have, so the distant dreams are just

that. My soul must be growing by leaps and bounds now, right Soul?

My Soul reassures:
Yes, we are growing and experiencing the present entries in our itinerary. Dreams can resurface as opportunities in the future for us, no worries.

Entry: Itinerary glimpse from The Angels of The Light:
You enjoy being a wife and mother—and two years later celebrate the birth of a son—this rounds off your little family nicely and you move three times as you visualize the perfect house coming to you—you settle in with your family and begin the busy activities of family life—with children growing and building social lives of their own.

My Mind questions:
A lot of fun family years, adventures, trip to Disneyland. *Is it really the more I have, the more I want or am I just anxious to experience life? Are other interests always pulling at me? Am I never satisfied?* This constant change is also part of growth, I am sure. Must settle now and count my blessings, need to feel connection to my path.

Entry: Itinerary glimpse from The Angels of The Light:
Your husband will appear distant from the family unit and family activities—you take a part-time job to be home for the kids—this job then turns into full time as the children grow—Mom's taxi service you are now providing as your daughter lands a summer job.

My Mind recognizes:
My family unit is changing; don't feel this change is normal though. *Does moving apart possibly bring us together?* I feel a magnetic draw pulling now. *Is this the best direction for my path? Will this enable real growth and maturity?* I am not feeling confident, have an unsettled feeling in my heart. *Am I going off track here?* The intuition hairs on my neck are standing up. *Is this the feeling of inner knowing? Could I be resisting a predetermined plan about the probable outcome or the inevitable?* What are you saying, wise Soul voice? Am I hearing your words in intuitive thoughts?

My Soul speaks:
Yes, I am sending intuitive thoughts to you, my Mind friend. It is time to stay alert to important choices of direction to our future of best. I will keep prompting you to select wisely.

My Mind wonders:
What can I do to foresee the future? I need to see the next entry, please. An insightful book on these changes and choices really would help my understanding about what is going on in my life. My understanding must be of utmost importance now! Clarity now would certainly help. I am really leaning on you, my Soul companion.

**A vision of self—
does open to self—
the ability to lift clarity of purpose—
and does engage the—
empowering of the journey—
... The Angels of The Light.**

Chapter Three:
Disillusionment—Mixed Emotions

Entry: Itinerary glimpse from The Angels of The Light:
You have developed a thirst for insight into the meaning of life and are compelled to fill your questioning and waiting time reading books—you ponder over thoughts about life—faith and the universe.

My Mind reflects:
Out on a Limb—book by Shirley MacLaine, this title fits how I am feeling. Change is definitely in the air, I sense my intuitive red flags are flying in front of my face. I am filling more of my time with girlfriend outings and less time being with my withdrawn husband. *Could there really be a good reason for this pulling apart?* Soul voice, where are you?

Entry: Itinerary glimpse from The Angels of The Light:
You attend your daughter's grade thirteen graduation ceremonies by yourself and proudly watch her receive her awards—enrolled in a big city college—you drive your daughter there and help settle all these novice roommates into their first apartment.

Disillusionment—Mixed Emotions

My Mind expresses:
My daughter's journey forward in her life. I have mixed feelings. I am excited for her and sad to be letting go of my baby girl so soon. Hoping I did my best in the role of mothering. Wish for her a spectacular life with quick insight of soul growth events.

Entry: Itinerary glimpse from The Angels of The Light:
Your husband has accepted a job transfer to this same big city of your daughter's college—the family home will be sold and you relocate—your son makes a choice to stay in his hometown to finish his last two years of high school—a temporary home for him to stay at is a very temporary fit.

My Mind reflects:
Sure hope my son's decision was a good one for him. *Is his maturity during these teen years flexible yet sustaining? Are my life events being controlled or guided here?* The writing is on the wall, I cannot dismiss these unsettled feelings. A door opens to the future, which direction to take? Life holds so many choices. *Could this all work out? Can I be sure at any time that the choice I make is the best one? Will I carry regrets forever for poor choices? Can positive soul growth come out of negativity, hurt, or revenge? Are we disconnected, Soul?*

Twenty years of marriage, I did not visualize it ending as it has. Lesson to self, I can only control my own choices; others have freedom of choice as well. Moving forward is the best medicine. *Wonder what events I have written in my soul growth itinerary to assist this movement.* A glimpse, a look, some understanding; yes, I need that now.

Entry: Itinerary glimpse from The Angels of The Light:
True self-discovery begins for you—you begin an unquenchable thirst to understand and gain insight about life along with the desire to shed the emotional baggage of a failed marriage.

My Mind reviews:
My ex-husband, my daughter, and I are now living in the same big city; however, we are somewhat estranged and living separate lives. *Can I justify my actions in an attempt to ease the ache? Are there verbal and unconscious commands that I am following now in an attempt to create calm or is it convenience? What kind of soul growth is this? Oh, this can be so confusing! Where to go from here? How do I start all over?* Am I not listening to your wise words, Soul?

My Soul engages:
Listen up here; things have a way of working themselves out. Pay attention to my promptings of future best choices. I am always here, stay open. Know that you are not alone on this journey. Keep this thought open to the lessons of the pressure you are imposing on yourself, my Mind friend.

My Mind questions:
Are you saying that I have hung up the open line of conversation we had engaged in previously?

My Soul confirms:
You have made a Mind decision to go it alone.

Disillusionment—Mixed Emotions

This is never a wise choice, as the insight of a team effort is so much more empowering. This happens when emotions lift to clutter your clear thinking and you forget that I am always here for our forward movement with insight. You do not hear my promptings, as the connection has been put on hold. This adventure is a together approach, an approach in ease of movement to express our mission in life here. I do not give up attempting to reach you, my Mind friend. So happy you are listening again.

**The placing of the rainbow—
at your fingertips—
we desire and do offer to you—
... The Angels of The Light.**

Chapter Four:

Spreading My Wings!

Entry: Itinerary glimpse from The Angels of The Light:
You accept a challenge and take on the adventure and travel to Europe with your roommate and long-time best friend—you both give up good career jobs in search of something more to life.

My Mind inquires:
Am I running away? Could this adventure also be an opportunity to reconnect with myself? Is it wise to place a new promising relationship on hold? Is it true that choices in life never end? I wonder, could this be my best choice for soul growth?

Entry: Itinerary glimpse from The Angels of The Light:
Your son is now in college and lives with his paternal grandparents in their hometown—two years of marriage separation now and your choices have presented a peripheral shock wave effect—your family will experience the damaging effects of an emotional roller coaster.

My Mind reflects:
Correspondence with my children from faraway places, can present new options to openly write to each other. *Could this choice have been a good one after all? Will my children be able to focus on their lives and school to remove the compelling notion of having to make a choice of which parent to show loyalty? Could my year of travel be beneficial to all involved?* I look forward to engaging in fun correspondence and sharing with my children. I am sure praying for this to be big soul growth. Time to let go and let God take over!

Entry: Itinerary glimpse from The Angels of The Light:
Your thirst for knowledge is engaged again—the new friendships with citizens of foreign lands feed your life perspective—your choice of travel companion and best friend is complementary and supportive as you share in each other's inner growth—you are sharing your adventure with your children and family—your new love interest chooses to visit you in a little village in the Swiss Alps to ring in the new year.

My Mind shares:
The fun of a totally new adventure lifts me to experience new cultures and a new perspective on life. Almost a year of travel adventures in Europe we have enjoyed. The comradely and enthusiasm of my travel companion, Lorraine is a refreshing experience. We memorize this inspiring phrase found in a magazine—*We have come from a time when we needed a partner just to survive; to a*

time when we can survive nicely on our own; and now in this present time, our partner's purpose is to Maximize our Joy! Okay, Soul, let's take on the future with my eyes wide open!

Entry: Itinerary glimpse from The Angels of The Light:
You return to Canada and pick up the pieces in an attempt to make wise choices for the future—your children and ex-husband are moving on to new beginnings in their lives and careers—you decide to train yourself for a new career in real estate sales—you accept the offer to take your college training in the hometown of your new man.

My Mind focuses:
I have a sense of moving forward with determination now; however, it is not without glitches. With every decision, there seems to be a spin off that affects others involved. Can this effect be labelled an *unsolicited and forced soul growth spin off,* for others? Can you explain this consequence effect Soul or Angels?

Entry: Itinerary glimpse from The Angels of The Light:
Your career is blossoming—you visualize the need for more personal space and independence—you proceed with divorce—you make a decision to go out on your own—buy a house and offer a reprieve to your new man with his challenges there—this is a surprise move to some—you take a short vacation alone to sort out your thoughts and travel to Australia to attend an Aussie girlfriend's

wedding—she is one of your roommates from Europe.

My Mind questions and reviews:
Why does this divorce after twenty years of marriage display resistance from my ex? *Is it not closure he wants? Am I to look back now for the soul growth from this union?* We did produce two wonderful children. I have grown to trust in myself and be responsible for my own happiness. I have observed the power of visualizing what I want and to be wise to what I want. I have become independent like my mother. I am not fearful of change and at times, I crave it. Gaining more intuitive insight and expressing my creativity has enabled me to embrace more self-respect. *However, are my choices for the future taking away the choice freedoms of others in my life? Can this be avoided when our lives are so interconnected?*

Lesson to self: I can never predict the reaction of others to the choices I make! Even if I believe my choice will display a possible beneficial gain of awareness for them. There is so much choice in life, it can be overwhelming! I am thinking it is important to take a moment to reflect. Do you have any comments, Angels?

The Angels respond:
Like the folds opening in sequence on the semicircle handheld fan—a quick review is displayed to assist the choice of this half-circle movement into action—we say here—the full vision of this half-circle is to release the pattern of old and refresh the choice with a new thought of best choice—the quick review is a

tool that is used to facilitate taking a moment to think about your next choice and to direct your thoughts and actions to the now as well as to the future there—this quick review is of assistance to carry to you an understanding to the importance of the next choice—this is usually offered when a pivotal direction is displayed—as within each fold of the fan opening example—this does offer and engage a shift in view or observation—the display is to past experiences as well as wisdom gained in the quickness of this unfolding display—it can offer the choice to journey of selection of best—or can offer the choice to journey of a status quo—and all aspects in between as free-will gift is maintained—as it is clear to you the choice of best—it may not be as clear to the observer of your actions and therefore—it can be of a process of gained understanding for their awareness to lift into this quick review—a level of alert awakened thought is required to gain in this refreshing quick review.

Entry: Itinerary glimpse from The Angels of The Light:
You are again searching for insight—books fill your spare time—they are pivotal for you as they offer insightful answers to your deepest questions.

My Mind reflects:
When I read something that rings the *truth bell* within me, this is my recognition of a higher powerful knowing of truth. *(You Will See It When You*

Believe It—by Dr. Wayne Dyer; Heal Your Body—by Louise L Hay; The Celestine Prophecy—by James Redfield.. these books offer intuitive answers to my questions) This feeling seems to resonate deep within me. *Is this my God connection? I must gain huge soul growth at these times. Can I then receive an insightful glimpse to my chosen path?* A heaping helping of clarity please.

My Soul engages:
It is wonderful to have you really listening again Mind. As your Soul companion, I am prompting you to the truth of our path and access to our ALL/God connection. This is the driving force and the glimpse of insight to gain clarity of the predesigned path. The floodgates of insight are opening. Prepare yourself for a very engaging adventure!

**We offer to you—
signs of our presence—
... The Angels of The Light.**

Chapter Five:

Grandchildren and Other Miracles

My Mind reflects:
I enjoy the feeling of helping others; this must be positive soul growth. *Is there negative soul growth?* I am praying for a thicker skin to enable me to stay in this present career. *Should I be careful what I wish for here?* A strong invisible (shatter-proof glass) shield needed now!

Entry: Itinerary glimpse from The Angels of The Light:
You become a grandmother to a precious baby girl—this gene recreation is an awesome and marvellous event of recognition for yourself and your daughter—you have more opportunities to bond again with your siblings and your mother as this baby is celebrated.

My Mind wonders:
Does time really mend hurts? Does a matured ability to process comments and events offer better choices with action rather than the reactive approach? Is this again my Soul growing? It's a magical feeling, this grandmother love and now four generations to celebrate. I cannot imagine a more joyous space than where I am right now.

What could possibly be waiting just around the corner?

Entry: Itinerary glimpse from The Angels of The Light:
You have a newfound sense of self with confidence—you are on the path of best—with this renewed inner strength— you attempt to remember to always protect your personal power—you joyously accept a marriage proposal.

My Mind comments:
Things seem to be happening for a reason, though they are not always clear to me. *Am I setting up more soul growth? Am I tuned in now or still rather oblivious to it all?* After almost a dozen years of courting, William proves to be the right Mr. Right. We marry and go to the west coast of Canada for our honeymoon. We experience the awesome magnificence of the Canadian Rocky Mountains, the Ice fields, many fabulous tourist attractions, and enjoyed visits with special friends throughout our travels in this province of British Columbia. A very enjoyable start to a second marriage for both of us.

Then I have a near-death experience; we miss our flight home; and experience a couple days of stand-by for connecting flights. *Does this require my heightened attentions now? Is this now a connected soul growth togetherness path of recognition? What is the correct answer?*

My Soul informs:
Your path is joined with your new husband only to

complement each other's focus of individual Soul growth. We will continue to take on this adventure together my Mind friend, as our own individual team.

Event: Itinerary glimpse from The Angels of The Light:
You have what is labelled there as a near-death-experience—while on your honeymoon— you experience this life review and visitation.

My Mind shares my Near-Death Experience:
My life is reviewing in my mind's eye; it takes me right back to childhood experiences and then relates these experiences to the current time in my life. While curiously watching this life movie, I am mostly unconcerned that my body is violently reacting and placing me into anaphylactic shock. I do recall a surprise sting while posing for photos at the totem pole display on Victoria Island. My husband seems to be in a panic to locate the nearest hospital. I am somewhat aware that I am gasping for air, yet my attention is calmly focused on my life review playing out within my mind. *Is this my time to leave earth? I am surprisingly okay with that thought!* This movie pauses at the times of big pivotal decisions in my life. It offers a reflection and the grasp of meaning or reason for events that happened. Very interesting! I am enjoying this elevated experience that appears to be lifting me into a light feeling of euphoria.

    Thoughts of my life being divinely guided enter my Mind. I have made good and not so good choices. I seem to be floating above myself and yet still am answering my new husband's questions. *Is this some kind of a split experience?* Part of me is here on earth, but another is holding or hovering and observing a vision of my life as if from a heavenly platform. *What is this space? Could this be the heavenly place we immediately go to upon death? Am I just visiting or actually dying?* Amazingly calm this space appears to have all the answers to my questions of life. I sense that important information is being told to me. *All is in perfect Divine Timing!* these words were spoken clearly and are a glimpse of information that now clings to my mind. I want to stretch my mind to embrace more information. *I need more time here!*

Oh no! Moments later, this loving and beautiful space seems to be gently yet definitely disappearing. *Or am I the one moving very fast?* I feel very safe, swirling, turning, and spinning. I am now feeling lightheaded and a bit dizzy. Then the swirling stops. My husband is standing on my left. I feel that I am still floating in happiness and smile at him. The space I was in had no walls to contain it. This room seems to somewhat mimic that space. I direct my focus on the end of my bed. *Hi, Doctor Steward,* I say calmly. These words seem to tumble out of my mouth.

Showing surprise he looks up at me, *How do you know my name?*

Oh, are you not the doctor who temporarily took on our family doctor's patients twenty or more years ago in my hometown in Ontario?

Yes I did, way back then! There must be nothing wrong with you young lady with a memory like that.

He moved to the side of my bed, putting the

clipboard down. With an expression of surprising coincidence, he continued to check my vital signs and said to rest awhile. He would write a prescription for an Epi-pen. The room seems more in focus now as I became aware of the walls and a privacy curtain at the end of my bed. It had appeared to my Mind that we are in a rectangular room and had been floating in air. Like a giant crane had hoisted this room to hang high above the ground. This hovering high in the sky sensation now changes as my Mind senses a gentle lowering action. Slowly I returned to terra firma. I feel very centered and alive. I also recognize an intense yearning to return to the place I had just visited.

My new husband engages me in conversation. I know he wants to be sure I am all right. Wow, an amazing experience! *Did I really almost die here? Is it true we have to be close to death to transform and really live life with renewed focus?* The doctor returns. I must carry this adrenalin cylinder with me from now on. It will give me extra time to reach help in case I experience another anaphylactic allergy attack, he explains.

What is the reason for this chance encounter with this Doctor from my past? Soul, please fill me in here. Nothing is haphazard I have heard. *Then what do I need to understand and retain here? Is there a message that ties into this near-death-experience? Soul, did you set this into our itinerary for a reason? A divine reminder and intervention? Wow an amazing experience!* I feel like I have just been given a huge heavenly hug. I remember these words—*Divine Timing!* Yes, that was what these Angels said—*All is in perfect Divine Timing!*

I have a strong sense that more of this heavenly information will return to my memory very soon. This out-of-body experience leaves me with a desire to discover more. Somewhat content for now to wait, I wonder when I will have full memory recall.

My Mind ponders whether a life review offers an opportunity to cleanse and mend emotional hurts. *Is a visit to the heavens the prelude to a huge shift in thinking? Is this also part of soul growth? Can it also offer an opportunity to gain wisdom, to make amends, to determine how to make better choices, to count my blessings, and to release the burden of blame? Am I sure it was a wise choice to sign up for this journey without full insight to begin with?* ALL IS WELL, describes the strong prompting I have lifting from deep within me. We return home from our honeymoon. A phrase continues to circulate in my thoughts; *Everything is as it is supposed to be!*

My Soul companion, what additional events have you prearranged for our future? *Could any future events possibly top this one?* A glimpse of the next step would definitely be of assistance to guide this Mind.

My Soul responds:
Yes, this is all part of our itinerary that I predesigned. This space you visited is filled with unconditional and total ALL love! It is all very logically and divinely orchestrated. Wait until you have further recollection of our Angel Visitation. That is just ahead now. Much more to discover on this team adventure here, my Mind friend.

**Our love surrounds and cradles you—
in the gentle rhythm of—
the wonders of The ALL—
... The Angels of The Light.**

Chapter Six:

A Happiness High

Entry: Itinerary glimpse from The Angels of The Light:
You experience the term—a happiness high—your mind opens to visually observe your first colourful recognition of a full-body aura—amazed by this visual earthly phenomenon—you begin research on its meaning.

My Mind engages:
A sight for my eyes! A colourful energy field began to appear to me, surrounding my body and also surrounding others. *Why have I not seen this before?* Also pets, animals, plants, and other objects have auras! Each colour band around the body holds meaning and displays our emotions with each colour change. This is amazing information! *Who knew? What else is seemingly hidden from my view?*

My Soul expands:
There are many more events scheduled and each one offers more insight to you, my Mind friend.

This insight on the human aura will assist you to observe our body's aura layers as well.

My Mind comments:
Soul voice, I hear you. There is so much to see in this somewhat invisible world that my Mind's vision is now transformed. It appears that I have opened up another compartment within my brain. A compartment labelled *Insightful tools for the Mind.* This compartment holds the directions and processes for gaining the ability to see aura fields. Consciously, I was not accessing this compartment. Awareness is now a wonderfully insightful ability.

Entry: Itinerary glimpse from The Angels of The Light:
You recognize the need for more balance in your lifestyle—you visualize your perfect job and life—you prepare a list of entries.

My Mind repeats and listens:
This is to resemble a descriptive list of my vision of a perfect job. Remember to describe everything about the item, my friend and real estate co-worker reads from *Do what you Love and the Money will Follow - by Marsha Sinetar.* Remember, not the item itself. List twenty descriptive points of my desired surroundings, needs, feelings, working hours, free time, emotional accomplishments, material gains, and inner gains. Think of your desire to help others, making a difference and leaving a mark on the world.

When this list is complete, present it in meditation to the universe. Trust now and believe in divine timing. These words *Divine Timing* appear to be surfacing in my life more often. Allow yourself to envision a seemingly impossible and magical descriptive to this job. There are no restraints, she says. Take as much time as you need, but finish this task.

Several weeks later, I had completed my list. Twenty items to describe the perfect job that would add the balance I had desired for my life. I allowed my mind to dream and be free of restriction. I detailed a magical and seemingly impossible job. It had vacation time, gains in self-motivation, and was financially rewarding. Even the hours of the day that I would perform this perfect job were noted.

I share my list with you here. At the time I was working as a real estate representative. The stress of the job, long hours, pager, phone, less time for me, without a feeling of balance in my life fed my desire to dream of change. In addition, my new husband worked shifts in his employment that left us vying for time together.

A Happiness High

My fantasy dream job:

- *To work for a large company that is positive-love based.*
- *Having branches all over the world.*
- *Freedom to express my individual talents.*
- *Allowing self-motivation (like self-employed work).*
- *Promotion of my talents.*
- *Encouraging, learning, and developing inner strength.*
- *Work 4–5 days a week. (6–8 hr. day)*
- *Weekends off regularly.*
- *Offers idea sharing—small group discussions.*
- *Working mostly out of my home office (where I can play my music, enjoy beauty, have flowers, and water nearby to walk to).*

- *Salary job/contract work—paid well.*
- *No pager required or call-in.*
- *Travel required to meet open and enlightened people. (3 x yr.)*
- *Holiday time when I want it.*
- *Other material gains and self-improvements.*
- *Feelings of love in my work and lightness in my heart.*
- *Time to work in my gardens.*
- *More free time to be with my new husband.*
- *Doing something that makes a difference in the world even in a small way.*
- *Help others using my own unique talents/gifts whatever they may be.*

Dream big is the suggestion, so I did. Hope this action opens doors, a new lifestyle, and a job to satisfy my need to make a difference. *This or something better is my wish!* I sent this wish out into the universe to manifest into my life.

Entry: Itinerary glimpse from The Angels of The Light:
You sit one afternoon in meditation—full helpings of joyful love have engaged and overflow into your life—being a new wife again—grandmother—stepmother—expression of gratitude is foremost in your thoughts as you visualize the approach of this blended family Christmas gathering.

My Mind agrees:
I am feeling so blessed that our blended family has merged so well. We are hosting a full family Christmas and I am looking forward to having time to hold and play with my new granddaughter. I must focus now as there is a lot of preparation to accommodate this large group celebration all at once in our little home.

My Soul voice is heard loud and clear:
Yes, your life is good and it continues to get better!

My Mind replies:
Is that your voice, Soul? I do want to keep our communication lines open. The busyness and stress of life seem to take over my thoughts, and I forget to talk with you. At times, I think that it is only me on this adventure. Sorry to ignore your promptings. I will reinforce my efforts to remain alert.

**The life journey is yours—
the light is always given.

The choice remains yours—
the focus we direct—
... The Angels of The Light.**

Chapter Seven:
Angel Visitation

Entry: Itinerary glimpse from The Angels of The Light:
You are visited by The Angels of The Light—you are reminded of your chosen mission—you begin the application of your mission.

My Mind tells all:
As Christmas was fast approaching, I found myself putting up decorations and reviewing the events and choices during the year. This recollection seemed to enhance a very joyful mood. Becoming a grandmother, my own new marriage, a near-death experience, seeing the seemingly invisible human aura, and an endless thirst for truth and knowledge seemed to present a synchronistic fit in my life. *Was I aware on some subconscious level that my several important choices would prepare me for what would happen next? Soul where you prompting my inner knowing?*

    I felt compelled to give thanks and express appreciation for this continuous *happiness high* in my life. The warmth and solitude of my little home on this sunny winter afternoon wrapped me in a comforting security. I began to meditate and voice my inner thoughts of gratitude to God, whom I

Angel Visitation

credited for this direction. *I am so grateful for your heavenly intervention in my life*, I expressed. Closing my eyes and focusing on a rhythmic breathing, the brilliant colours floated into my mind's eye. I relaxed further and continued my expression of gratitude for the joy in my life. Then my focus changed. I wanted to initiate an idea for a creative special gift that would touch my new husband with love.

I really enjoy using this stress-relieving tool of meditation in my life now. That meditation course I took is paying off big time. However, my creative mind seemed to be asleep on this task request as no special gift ideas were surfacing. After a few minutes of empty thoughts, I decided to return to this meditation another time.

Suddenly as I moved to stand up, a loud crack sound echoed in the room. Or was it heard just in my ear? This soul-stirring sound appeared as if to gain my attention to announce the three words that I heard next. A very deep baritone male voice seemed to fill the space of my home and spread within my mind and body. It engulfed the room and enveloped the whole house in this singular moment. The sound of these words seemed to materialize and bounce off the walls. The three words I heard were: **DRAW HIS ANGEL!** A startling suggestion to me!

What? Who? Where? Why? I am alone here, am I not? Startled! Surprised! Shocked! Fearful! My reaction was immediate with these unsettling emotions and thoughts. However, the house appeared so serenely still, similar to the stillness during my near-death experience earlier this year.

Then a wonderful sense of peace consumed my thoughts, allowing me to accept that what was happening in my space…*WAS ALL OKAY.*

Instinctively I moved to search for the art pad and chalk pastels I had purchased on a whim several months earlier. I had only retrieved these items a week prior from temporary storage in at my stepdaughter's home. *A beyond co-incidence synchronicity?* Sitting down calmly with this art pad openly resting on my knee and a pencil held upright over this pad, I returned to meditation and waited. *Could what was about to happen next possibly be familiar to me?*

However, my reaction was again immediate disbelief when the pencil began to write out words on the paper. Jumping up, knocking both pad and pencil to the floor. I was not able to accept this! *How can this be happening to me?* The first of several questions sprang into my heightened attention. *Who are you?* While pondering these disturbing thoughts and pacing the room, time seemed to stand still. As I began feeling somewhat more in control of the situation or trying to convince myself of this, I retrieved the pad and pencil. I cautiously sat back down, forcing myself to regain my composure. *How much time had actually passed or did it stand still?* I can only guess, as feelings of safety and comfort were again filling me in a familiar way. *Who Are You? What Are You? Why are you doing THIS—TO ME?* These questions and more tumbled out, my curiosity standing alert now and my impatience for answers showing. The pencil moved again very slowly; these words were written and also given to me in thought. **We are The**

Angel Visitation

Angels of The Light—we would like to bring a loving message to your husband through you and draw his Angel. We will move slowly and keep you in our safe love.

My willingness to comply with this request must have registered quickly. I relaxed again into meditation. The writing began and continued, signing off with the name of my husband's Angel. Then the page seemed to flip over on its own initiative. A drawing began, as my hand appeared directed to drop the pencil and pick up pastel chalk pieces from the open box beside me. Moving quickly with intent, colours were selected and applied in guided strokes onto the art paper. Then this action stopped. I cautiously opened my eyes. Displayed before me was a multi-coloured and decidedly reflective Angelic presence. *This is amazing! What have I just experienced? Has this actually happened to me?*

Now what? This last thought abruptly disturbed my awe of this breathtaking and unfolding experience.

Wrap it up as a gift for your husband! A suggestion was clearly received in my conscious mind. However, I immediately questioned this wisdom. My husband is a truly sceptical person by nature. This gift may seem inappropriate to him, I rationalized. My logical mind needed some time to process and think this through. However, I did choose to wrap it up. Then I hid it under other gifts behind the Christmas tree. *Out of sight—out of mind!* A funny thought for me, as it is one of my husband's sayings. Guess his sayings are rubbing off on me.

The next couple of weeks I was absorbed in attempts to rationalize what had happened. I tried to reinforce the nagging doubts with reluctance to acknowledge that I have been singled out by Angels and given this gift of communication. *Who could I talk to without ridicule?* I am hearing invisible voices! Endless questions surfaced. *I NEEDED REAL PROOF!* The seemingly indisputable wisdom of the answers I received from these Angels of The Light compelled me to question further. Signs were given to me daily. A surreal closeness to the energy of these Angels suspended me and I gently moved into a leap of faith! *How could I not comply with this Angel request?* **Give him this gift—he has so much to gain and you have nothing to lose!**

Christmas Eve arrived and my mood was joyful calmness as I handed the last gift to my husband. With only a brief outline of how it came about. I told him it was a specially requested gift. With inquisitive glances at me, he gingerly unwrap this Angel portrait and messages as if expecting something to jump out at him. Surprised and encouraged by his immediate reaction and comment, I began to fill him in on the details of my experience. *I am not sure how to react to this gift,* he said tentatively. *However, I am touched that you wanted to do something very special for me!* Relief filled my mind and anxiety dissolved after hearing his honest response. My original desire of a special gift to express my love to him was accomplished with extraordinary heavenly assistance!

My Soul speaks:
How is that for something special!

My Mind replies:
Soul voice, you sound gleeful and the volume is turned way up to engage me. I am hearing you loud and clear, my friend.

My Soul responds:
This gift of Angel communication will guide you, my Mind companion, into full understanding of our journey here. Acceptance of it will be empowering!

My Mind reports:
This event is something I don't believe I could ever have imagined! Where will our life journey lead next, Soul? Working with Angels is an unbelievable magical job. Further conversations with my husband are inevitable. His Angel portrait was the initiating presentation from The Angels of The Light to awaken him. So many more questions and signs of proof will be needed to open him up further, I am sure. However, it is said that—*when the student is ready—the teacher will appear!* I know it has definitely awakened me to my mission recognition!

**We do seek here to assist—
and guide your every step—
into the joy of life—
... The Angels of The Light.**

Chapter Eight:

Name Meaning and Mission Confirmation

Overview Mission—Mission/Purpose—Focus Requirement—Intended Directive—Desired Support

My Mind confirms:
My courage grew to speak openly of this event to selected friends. As Angel portraits and messages were presented to curious family and friends, my confidence grew to allow me to welcome whatever delightful adventure was waiting to come into my life. The uniqueness of the Angel portraits and acknowledged accuracy of the guiding messages continued to be agreeable to me. Tender unconditional love was written within these messages. The recipient of each reflective portrait appeared to be emotionally touched. A visual Angelic connection presented an instant recognition for some. The response was repetitive of the magic offered within each Angel portrait I channelled. Individual observations of a refreshed and uplifted awareness endorsed the empowerment offered by the Angels through these personal connections.

Name Meaning and Mission Confirmation

Entry: Itinerary glimpse from The Angels of The Light:
You will receive confirmation of your chosen life mission—it is displayed to you in what appears as a somewhat hidden subconscious fit—when you recognize the signal of truth within your soul—this confirmation signal gives you a glimpse of your path with more confidence—you will become aware of your Overview Mission as it applies to your Intended Purpose to assist a successful achievement of soul growth with a Directive Approach.

My Mind questions:
Should I have been more leery or doubting when my Guardian Angels of The Light tell me that I chose this mission? That I was clever as many other souls are and even chose my name for its meaning. That I bonded with my parents, whom I also chose! That I also suggest my first name to my parents prior to birth, by accessing this energy bonding experience.

The Angels went on to say that my parents retain their gift of free-will. Should they choose not to give this suggested name as the new baby's first name, it is usually given as a second name or nickname. I chose to birth into the Messenger family for the experience I would gain. That this experience would certainly assist me on this life mission I chose. Then the Angels of The Light suggested for me to do some detective work: **Search out the meaning of your names to gain confirmation of your chosen life mission!** This directive was given and clearly received as a response to my question: *Why would I choose my parents and my name?*

Total surprise! The uncanny description of my name was discovered within the pages of library books interpreting name meanings and their origins. I was curious yet not prepared for this revelation to the meaning within my name. **Gloria** *means Celebration, Joy, Angel Love—and Angel.* **Messenger** *means - Deliverer of an Important Message - as well as Angel.*

This literally spells out my mission, just as The Angels predicted. **Celebrate the joy of Angel love and deliver this important message!** The Angels confirm this statement. *Do life's mysteries unravel for each of us as we become more alert and aware of our somewhat hidden clues?*

We have embedded clues within our lives, waiting to be discovered. *Does this enable us to make better choices on our earthly paths when we uncover these clues?* As the New Year began, my enthusiasm for life seemed to lift also. Courage surfaced with ease as a decision to change careers and work from my home led me to more self-confidence in my ability to create my dream lifestyle. *Remember my list for a dream job?* The first and second items I wrote down popped into my thoughts: *To work for a large company that is positive love-based* and secondly *for that company to have branches all over the world.*

My Soul states with emphasis:
Where could there be a larger company that is more positive love-based with branches all over the world? What could be bigger than The ALL Source/God/Creator's infinite unconditional love and that

this love is ever-present around the world? You were open to my promptings when you compiled this list for your dream job, my Mind companion.

My Mind agrees as it grasps this insight:
Amazingly, or should I say with no lingering doubt, so true! The balance of my items can also be checked off. *It all fits the life I now enjoy!* Yes, I do hear you clearly, Soul. These synchronistic events are showing up in my life consistently and frequently. *This goes way beyond coincidence!*

OVERVIEW MISSIONS:

Entry: Itinerary glimpse from The Angels of The Light:
You will be given the five Overview Life Missions—these you will share with others to assist their mission recognition: SHARE—EXAMPLE—INSPIRE—TEACH—HEAL.

My Mind engages:
So interesting, an overview of our life mission!

My Soul adds:
Our Overview Life Mission is to INSPIRE, my Mind friend. This we are to offer to others in the work that does drive and motivate us. It fuels our intended purpose and assists our directive approach. In other words it propels our chosen mission for this soul growth adventure.

My Mind questions:
Oh, that seems a bit too powerful to attain. *Have we taken on too much? To inspire others!* Soul, can we really achieve such a lofty overview mission?

My Soul continues:
NO PROBLEMS just follow my lead. This chosen Overview Mission word can be compared to a revved up engine empowering our journey

here. Acceptance of this insight will give us the empowerment needed to achieve our intention of soul growth. This is definitely our Overview Mission, my Mind friend. We will present it together.

My Mind listens to absorb:
Okay, I will allow this to absorb into my Mind. As long as you are on board my travelling partner. I will need direction to focus and stay open to hear your voice and prompting. I am guided to look up the meaning of *inspire* in the dictionary. Its meaning: *To exert an invigorative influence upon a person; to direct or guide as if by special divine influence.* My thoughts are watchful.

What is an Overview Mission?

The Angels of The Light describe further:
Overview Missions are described as an observation of intent—what a soul desires to achieve in the area of growth—with the assistance of an invisible empowerment—this invisible empowerment is driven by the ALL Source—and is gifted as a helping hand—to offer an example here—the Overview Mission is the engine that drives—or like a covering of an umbrella that encompasses the intention to every task undertaken by the soul—to ensure success in soul growth—it is your first choice made prior to incarnation when preparing your itinerary—it acts as a simplistic one word-motivating clue as it is descriptive of the original soul growth goal—this focused intention is the built-in motivator you receive to facilitate assisting others—while applying it to your everyday tasks—as well as your

Name Meaning and Mission Confirmation

interaction with other souls you encounter on your predesigned itinerary.

My Mind remains impressed:
Sounds important! I must now memorize our mission beginning with this Overview word. Would be great to have a go-to statement to align with and highlight our best choices. As it is our teams' motivating word to offer assistance to others, I appreciate any promptings from you, wise Soul. This Mind now engages in memorizing our mission statement, starting with—TO INSPIRE OTHERS—TO CELEBRATE THE JOY OF ANGEL LOVE—AND DELIVER THIS IMPORTANT MESSAGE!

   Do life's mysteries unravel for me (the Mind) as I become more alert and aware of the clues embedded within our journey together here? What discovery is next, my Soul companion? Is there more to discover with our names?'

My Soul responds:
Yes, middle names also hold clues. The Angels of The Light will explain further.

The Angels of The Light add further:
The middle names hold clues to offer a description of how to maintain your personal energies—this is then a Focus Requirement on the needs of your form or body—as momentum is engaged with application of your soul growth Overview Mission and your descriptive Intention Purpose.

My Soul adds:
Our middle name's somewhat hidden clue is *to a feminine self-preservation*, my Mind friend!

Your middle name *Wilma, is a female version of William which means—the resolute protector.* This interprets to promote a maintaining of our personal team energies in a feminine way.

My Mind repeats:
In a feminine self-preservation, to protect my personal energies! Well, that sounds like fun spa trips ahead. Thanks for the additional insight, Soul. Is there more?

My Soul engages:
And the answer is—YES! There is still so much more insight and assistance available to engage on this adventure we take together. Hope you continue to enjoy fabulous surprises, my Mind friend.

The Angels of The Light continue:
There are also hidden clues held within the Marriage Names one chooses to accept— these marriage name clues are attached to your previous name meaning in the after- support to your mission direction—these marriage name meanings hold for you a desire to observe and experience the descriptive traits to add enhancement to your mission— these additional names are termed Desired Support.

OUR TOTAL MISSIONS: Overview Mission— our Mission-Purpose—a Focus Requirement— an Intended Directive— and Desired Support within married names.

My Mind reflects:
Need to put this all together for my understanding and retention in my Mind's knowledge compartment.

Name Meaning and Mission Confirmation

There are now FIVE parts to our predesigned Life Mission or Purpose. I list here to improve comprehension.

Overview Mission: —one of five choices! (my team choice—*to Inspire others*)

Mission/Purpose: —first name! (my first name choice suggestion = *to Celebrate the Joy of Angel Love*)

Focus Requirement: —middle names! (my choice of middle name = *a feminine Self-Preservation*)

Intended Directive: —birth surname! (my surname choice = *to Deliver this Important Message*)

Desired Support: —observe traits within the married surnames! (my choice of marriage names = *to observe a Reinforced Self-Preservation and to observe a Preservation of Life Balance*)

My Soul confirms:
You got it, Mind! Now the complete confirmation and observation of our chosen mission on this adventure of growth is obviously gaining clarity to you.

My Mind responds:
All these choices of names are so very clever of you, Soul. I am so impressed how each has held clues to offer a lifting of the veil of forgetfulness. This is truly an insightful directive for our journey onward together here. Your attention to detail prior to this incarnation birthing will surely continue to amaze!

My Soul entices:
You know what I am going to continue to say as this book is guided by The Angels of The Light. There is still SO MUCH MORE!

**It is of joyful celebration—
we connect with you—
… The Angels of The Light.**

Chapter Nine:
Granddaughter's Angel Vision!

My Mind explains:
Christmas arrived again with all its blessings after a swift passing of eventful months. Then as another New Year began, my enthusiasm for life continued to lift. Courage and confidence surfaced with ease to reinforce the decision to further express my work with the Angels. The lifestyle of my dreams awaits my acceptance.

I was feeling very touched, humbled, and grateful as thank you cards, shared stories, angel gifts, and endorsing words from others came in the mail. Empowerment was the fuel to circulate these emotional stories into print I visualized. The next evening I received another gentle push.

Divine Timing —these two words replayed in my mind. *Heavenly guidance at work again?*

My Mind listens:
Tingles of inner knowing went up my spine as I listened to my daughter Sharon's words over the phone. *Mom, you're not going to believe what just happened!* She continued to relate the details of her experience with my little granddaughter that very evening. It was bath time and two-and-a-

Granddaughter's Angel Vision!

half-year-old Alyssa was drying off, wrapped in a towel, cuddling on her mother's lap. They began the routine of singing a lullaby song—*Rock a bye baby on the tree top*, when Alyssa interrupted the singing.

Look, Mommy, an Angel!

Staring at the area did not reveal an Angel vision to my daughter's eyes. However she questioned further watching the actions of her daughter. It was clear that this little one was seeing an Angel. Alyssa continued to watch the Angel that was in the bathroom with them.

It's up there, Mommy! She pointed continuing to focus on the spot just above the mirror lights.

What is it doing? Sharon asked.

Alyssa sung her response—*It is twirling around and around!*

Is it a boy Angel or a girl Angel?

It is a man Angel, Mommy!

Is it saying anything to you? Sharon inquired.

Alyssa cuddled shyly into her mother's arms. *It says, I WUV YOU!* she answers with a giggle.

To the family's amazement, my little granddaughter has repeated these words to others over the years in startling detail. At the tender age of four, she has drawn a colourful crayon picture of this Angel Vision to share with us. *(it is shared here in black and white)*

A Mirroring Discovery with Angel Visitation—Gloria Messenger

Alyssa's Angel

My Mind continues:
I remain so very touched to experience children talking about the Angel visions they experience. *Could we as adults become determined to re-engage our ability to see the seemingly invisible?*

My Soul comments:
Grandchildren are such blessings—and young children in particular are readily able to see Angel energies. They are free from the controls of what is possible and not possible in life until they assimilate into the teachings of society around age five or six. She had not yet received teachings that instruct an opposite suggestion about our ability to see an Angel. This shared experience will ignite the possibilities of visual angel viewing for others.

**Your path is filled with wonder—
and also a learning in joy—
... The Angels of The Light.**

Chapter Ten:

My Story Takes Flight

Overview Missions—Emotional Pulse—Balance/Off-Balance

My Mind formulates:
From the mouths of babies! *A heavenly boost?* The Angel Awareness newsletter was born and launched and seemingly took flight around our world. The Angelic encounter stories began to pour in and the initial circulation expanded perpetually. Popularity beyond expectation was my experience with each printing.

My husband and I delighted in seeing the return addresses and postage in our mailbox. These letters arrived from near and distant towns, cities, and countries, expressing their own emotional awe of the personal messages they received within their channelled Angel portraits. The mirroring reflection was compelling to them and this was offered further with each viewing revelation.

Observation of this newsletter circulation appeared inexhaustible, especially after my Angel encounter story was published and spread internationally. The Angel Awareness newsletter worked its magic, and my journey continues to be guided with many ways to deliver this Angel message.

My Soul interjects:
It is impressive how you are grasping this insight, my Mind friend. I will continue to offer repetition to solidify this insight within your retention memory. Oh YES, there is still more to experience on our pre-planned itinerary!

My Mind reviews:
When I take a mind review of what has happened since the Angels of The Light visited during my *meditation of gratitude*, it is a journey of wonderful surprise. Amazing insights, as well as heavenly guidance with each step forward continues to be my new norm. Listening for my Soul voice has become an ingrained habit and wonderful feeling to know that this adventure is a joint effort. Gratitude was the intent to express then and continues to be the focus on this journey of soul growth that I have signed up for. Curiosity leads onward and any glimpse of insight is exciting and still amazes me.

The Angels of The Light continue:
To engage an easier understanding and recognition of ones' Overview Missions— we offer here all five mission aspects with balance and off-balance approaches.

With application of the Emotional Pulse taken—one can aspire to an elevated level— with applied expression to self and others.

**SHARE—the positive *Emotional Pulse application will reveal—*A desired focus to offer information to assist others choices.*

However—when the focus to this Overview mission strays—an **off-balance is evident in application—*then feelings of being copied—requiring a favour to be returned or strings attached to sharing self—a feeling of being drained—or feeling unappreciated—*can be observed.

EXAMPLE—the positive *Emotional Pulse application will reveal—*A desire to formulate plans and details to show or assist others.* However—when the focus to this Overview mission strays—an **off balance is evident in application—*then thoughts are occupied with how events should play out—a berating of self—a goal driven rather than a Soul-driven focus—*can be observed.

INSPIRE—the positive *Emotional Pulse application will reveal—*A desire to change or reshape the world for the better.* However—when the focus to this Overview mission strays—**off balance is evident in application—*thoughts of vulnerability—desire to flee problems—desire for respect from others to validate self—*can be observed.

TEACH—the positive *Emotional Pulse application will reveal—*A desire to challenge and expand upon accepted thoughts.* However—when the focus to this Overview mission strays—**off balance is evident in application—*thoughts of insufficient acknowledgment received of one's acquired wisdom and or higher education—desire and need for accolades—*can be observed.

HEAL—the positive *Emotional Pulse application will reveal—*A desire to offer a healing approach to improve the body of humanity.* **However—when the focus to this Overview mission strays—**off balance is evident in application—***insatiable seeking for respect of ability—desire to personally control outcome—no welcoming of assistance or team effort—***can be observed.**

*Emotional Pulse *(Intuitive Inner Pulse)*
The Angels of The Light explain:
Emotional Pulse*—in the positive is observed when one's inner knowing is heard** *(little truth voice in your head)* **and recognition of a state of peace fills the body—this could also be termed an Intuitive Inner Pulse—that offers guidance to our choices in life—it is a lifted feeling of your truth as is evident in the emotions you are experiencing.**

**Off Balance:
The Angels of The Light explain:
** *Off Balance***—begins with recognition of being Off Balance—negative thoughts occupy the mind with personal insecurities—there may be a repetitive dialogue that stalls forward movement—one is off-balance and off the intended path—make a shift from imbalanced to a positive balanced Emotional Pulse—encouragement to meditate—pray for one's return of faith energies in the ALL love— will enable the re-engagement of the positive approach to the chosen Overview Mission—an elevated level of insight is the gain when the**

awareness is engaged to remain in balance and thereby observe one's inner truth—then lifting the mind into clarity.

My Mind focuses:
S E I T H = to see it! Sounds like old Elizabethan English. This anagram *SE-ITH* encourages some visual prompting to comprehend. Overview Missions we have chosen in the initial stage of preparing our uniquely individual itinerary. We can see that there is so much included to keep us on path here. Now we have this Observation of Intent. We can come to recognize when we are off balance by taking our emotional pulse. I am impressed and grateful for this added support and directive. Continuously amazing!

My Soul replies:
This anagram stands for our ability to see this overview mission driving us forward here. When the itinerary is prepared, a focus to detail is emphasized for our team motivation. Can you see my friend?

My Mind collects:
Okay, now I can recognize when I am off balance with my Overview Mission. I cannot *inspire others* when I am out of harmony with my mission intent. These descriptions of being emotionally off balance truly fit me. I know when I do not feel centered within. My energy is also low and this is another clue to check my emotional pulse. This is so empowering for me, the Mind in this travelling team arrangement to quickly recognize the clues of being off balance.

Entry: Itinerary glimpse from The Angels of The Light:
You will be shaken and think you are being tested when your husband becomes very ill— this experience will be for his benefit more so than yours.

My Mind expresses:
I am feeling emotionally vulnerable from the severity of his illness. Vulnerable because the doctor tells me *that he may not survive* and emotional because *I want to trust and believe that all will be well. What could be the meaning for this?* As my worry heightens, I am also encouraged daily by my husband's lifted faith in the outcome. His daily renewed determination to overcome his health challenge is encouraging. Although, could he be putting on a good optimistic front for me as well? He tells the family not to worry. Prayers are sent out by all concerned. A miracle occurs and he is gradually taken off all medications!

The doctors say, *You are a miracle man! This disease usually claims life within a short time!* He is described as an A-typical patient in the response to the control and run of this disease. I believe he still has a mission to fulfill here on earth.

What is my lesson to be learned from his illness? *I must remain self-trusting of my faith, knowing that it will hold and empower me as I step forward through the events of life*? My emotional pulse of feeling very vulnerable and off-balance has definitely been on display.

My Soul enlightens:
As we venture forth together, the focus of this joint

preservation is reinforced when the life of a loved one is in jeopardy. We all have the will and the power to overcome obstacles in our path. I confirm here, strong faith can engage miracles.

The Angels of The Light offer encouragement:
Have strength—full steps forward—you are not alone—it is in this joyful knowing that The ALL light shines brightly and sustains—we all assist and embrace you.

My Mind reflects:
It sure does not hurt to be comforted while talking to my Angels. I really like having these miracle-maker friends in high places, always with me. I mean with us, Soul. I hear your comments of insight. Thank you.

My Soul offers:
As we continue this journey together, comfort will always be offered by our Angels to assist insight, with a push to remember what this journey is all about. I will lift to you awareness and observations; you just have to remain alert, my traveling companion.

My Mind is thankful:
I am so grateful, Soul voice. Really need to know you are so very close to me. Want to always be alert to your presence and wise guidance.

**The gentle touch—
reaches deep within—
to offer you brilliance—
of glistening clarity—
... The Angels of The Light.**

Chapter Eleven:

Linking with Our Angels

Event: Itinerary glimpse from The Angels of The Light:
You will become more aware that your Angels are always near.

My DREAM Vision:

My Mind remembers:
The memory of a dream or vision is replayed in my mind as I wake: — A giant bumblebee *(the size of a baseball)* is buzzing in front of my face. It hovers in place for a few minutes allowing me to notice a miniature Angel *(the size of Disney's Tinker-Bell)* that is sitting on this bee's back. The wings of the Angel are folded between the bee's wings as this Angel appears to be fully enjoying this unique ride. Once given the opportunity to focus on this remarkable vision for a moment, the Angel smiles and waves as they fly away. My dream ends.

What message of guidance is lifted here? Can you help me interpret this dream, Soul companion?

My Soul answers:
A dream to lift and stimulate your memory recall is the interpretation.

Linking with Our Angels

My Mind expands:
Soon afterward, it is brought to my attention that the hardworking bumble bee is considered an aerodynamic mystery-miracle. The body shape and size, compared to the size of the little wings, defies all the basic principles of modern aviation. This bumble bee is not supposed to be able to fly! It is definitely a mini-miracle-mystery! And a truly interesting connection when I recall that a sting put me into anaphylactic shock, that led me to experience an amazing space I believe to be heaven were I was embraced with the euphoric feeling of receiving a group Angel hug. *Miracles defy logic! Is that the message?* Love to hear your comments, Soul voice.

My Soul offers:
You have glimpsed the space of heaven. You are beginning to recall your visit to heaven in more detail now. Prepare to meditate on this dream and enjoy where it guides you.

My Mind recalls:
My next meditation transports me back in the space of suspended all encompassing love. I am intently observing this expansive view of spectacular multi-coloured uninterrupted splendor. Beauty appears to occupy every object. *This must be heaven I am visiting!* Just like previously the distant edges of this vision are contained with a transparent sheet of white veil or curtain that moves in a gentle breeze. This gives me containment acceptance to the space in front of me, yet offers what appears to be never-ending scenery beyond it. There are light beings in a group standing close and facing me.

They appear translucent and iridescent in many colours yet quit solid as they move to embrace me in a huge group hug. I feel overwhelmingly euphoric pure love from this embrace! This truly is an Angel hug! I do not want it to end and feel no need to rush this intimate experience. I realize that instruction and encouragement from this group of light beings is transferring to me. This information is important and I accept the guidance received, you *will retain and recall all this information with Divine timing*. Those words again, *Divine Timing!*

Now these beings of light move back to display the splendor of their magnificent wings. I will never become tired of this heavenly vision. The powerful display again takes my breath away. Their wings radiate in translucent shades of blues and the space surrounding their wings becomes engaged in a brilliant illuminating golden aura. Even more astounding this time! If this magnificence is only a glimpse of heaven, it is beyond my ability to completely describe. These Angels are truly majestic beings! They command my full attention with their size, their iridescent colours, and the euphoric expression of love that fills this space they occupy.

A chorus of Angel song is ever-present. The perfection of the musical sounds I hear is alerted to my attention, especially now that they appear to be fading away. The Angels are still with me, yet they also appear to be receding out of my focus. *NO, NOT AGAIN! I clearly remember this feeling. It is the same sensation of instant home-sickness!* This emotion of withdrawal I instantly remember from my previously near-death-experience while celebrating our honeymoon. I want to stay and engage in conversation with these heavenly Angel beings. *ALL IN TIME—DIVINE TIMING!* These words linger with me.

I am aware that I am lifting from my meditation. However this time with a strong sense that the important information has been stored in my Mind for quick retrieval. Soul, what do you want to add to this revisiting of heaven experience?

My Soul offers:
This love permeates everywhere in a never-ending Omni presence, delivered by Angels. Just keep open to recall the Angel guiding messages as they highlight them, my Mind companion. I will prompt and assist our every step.

My Mind becomes excited:
Linking with my Guardian Angels will be an empowering tool. I learn that the Angels reach out to us by accessing our six senses. A sign or a clue to best choices on this life path would be wonderfully and personal connection to their insight. With memory recall surfacing, this Mind energy of our team is encouraged and excitedly anticipating more clarity. How can I openly connect with my Angels?

How to Link and connect with Our Angels:

The Angels of The Light offer this guidance:
Begin by inviting us into your thoughts—ask for assistance to celebrate your true self—relax in meditative quiet space and open your energy connection by taking several deep breaths and releasing slowly—take

a leap of faith and transcend doubt—if for only a moment—that you will connect here with us—your Angels—select a signal or sign from one of your six senses—Vision—Smell—Sound—Taste—Touch—Intuition—as you continue to breathe in a relaxed manner you are mixing the energies of heaven and earth—now describe to us—your Angels how you would like to be alerted to this access—a link of communication with you—ask for understanding—insight—and clarity—soak up the feelings of lightness as you are in the presence of The ALL love—okay—now go about your life—we will be in contact.

When we show our link with you—be alert to our messages of guidance from The ALL Source—become aware of your thoughts—are they positive or negative thoughts you are entertaining—become aware to your surroundings—observe the beauty around you or is a caution required—also what did you just hear—wise words from a friend—it is always in your immediate environment—we reach out to you in many ways—the Angel link-up may reveal an action is needed—it could be a confirmation that you are on the right path—your thoughts are confirmed—or this is the correct choice—and it may also be a presentation to you to take your time and gather more information—you will receive an inner knowing of what is applicable—ask for clarity—your chosen link-up will be accessed by us to offer guidance to you there on your chosen path.

Linking with Our Angels

My Mind follows up:
Choosing a link with my Angels by selecting one of my six senses is the first step. The six senses of:— Vision—Smell—Sound—Taste—Touch—Intuition. *Okay, I choose the sense of Touch.* Describe how I would like my Angels to access this link or clue to me of their presence. *Okay, tickle me on my face, Angels.* I begin to invite my Angels into my thoughts and ask for assistance to celebrate my true self as I visualize opening my energy connection to them. I take several deep breaths, releasing slowly and relaxing. Now transcending my doubts is next. *What do I have to lose; this could be a wonderful tool of assistance.* I continue a slow rhythm of breathing in and visualize that I am mixing the energies of heaven and earth. This is an engaging and thought-provoking vision for me. *Angels, please tickle me on the face around my cheeks and nose, I rephrase my request.* I ask now for *understanding, insight, and clarity.* Am I really feeling a lightness of being and possibly an Angel Hug? This is a wonderful feeling!

   I am anxious for my first contact. My Angels will use this link to give me awareness of their presence while I go about my life. When the *Angel Alert sign* is prompted to my recognition, *they want to alert me to my thoughts, my surroundings, to share a confirmation that I am making the best choice, or that more information needs to be gathered to make the best choice.* Now I just wait for this recognition.

   Thank you, Angels. I have come to recognize my link-up sign with you and intuitive lifting of your message. I am very grateful for this wonderful assistance and this open Angel Alert connection in my life.

My Mind expands:
I continue with clarity of my desires and the conversation with my Angels expands. I know that now with the Angels' presence in my life, I can ask the questions that I have buried a long time ago. I can make the time to connect with them in a gentle open approach as I would with my very best friend. I have also found that taking time for meditation, counting my blessings with expression of gratitude, with the intent focus, to reach out and inspire the Angel love, seems to lift my soul voice into a loving sound of guidance to my inner ear. I feel so blessed to have this open connection with my Angels, the Vibrations of The ALL love.

Being thrown off balance on this journey at times, I know that it is—*to be human*. When I have disconnected from my Angels, for reasons that are important at the time, yet seem so unimportant to me when I recognize my position of being off balance, I quickly reconnect. My Angels are patiently waiting for me and usually I quickly recognize my wayward ways with my first signal of a heavenly tickle. Then stopping myself to remember to reconnect, I am amazed at how joyful their work is. Also, the recognition of being touched by the genuine love from the heavens is empowering! *I know they are working through me on my intention focus.*

My Soul reinforces:
As your Soul companion on this journey we share, it is of awareness that assists a quick recovery and

return to our chosen path. With Angel assistance always available for the asking, the direction of best choice is highlighted in synchronistic scenarios to offer clarity. Accessing the Angel guidance offered on our journey is team empowering and I will also provide intuitive promptings of an inner voice of truth, my Mind friend.

My Mind replies:
Thanks for the promptings and the companionship. It is wonderful to never feel alone on this journey or adventure in life. You are what I term *a keeper* on this team to achieve success of the intended soul growth. What can you offer me in glimpses, my dear Soul companion?

My Soul expresses:
I cannot be booted off the team, so that justifies the term *keeper*. You can ignore me, dismiss my promptings, and totally tune me out. However, we travel together whether the awareness of the team is acknowledged or not. It is certainly a more pleasant journey to be acknowledged and listened to, being contained as I am within this body. An open awareness offers up the phrase —*that time flies because we are having fun*. More fun to come!

Event: Itinerary glimpse from The Angels of The Light:
You have received an Angel Hug poem from The All and The Angels of The Light—you will have opportunity to share this love embrace with many on your path now.

My Soul relates:
In the wee hours of the morning, I am awoken

to receive automatic writings from my Angels. I share this poem as received in 2001. Enjoy a visual embrace or physically wrap your arms around yourself to sense the pressure embrace of an Angel Hug. Repeat these words aloud or to yourself.

The Angels of The Light offer this hug:

> **I begin in this moment to
> embrace myself in love.**
>
> **To open my heart to touch my Soul truth—
> and—let my Angels in!**
>
> **To look for the gem in each
> and every moment.**
>
> **To release past hurt and fear—and let it go!**
>
> **To harmonize my life and allow my
> Soul to sing—I let my Angels in!**

My Mind comments:
I have witnessed the impact this poem has had on others and the joy I receive from sharing it. Thank You, Angels!

My Soul confirms:
A very satisfying mission choice—if I do say so myself!

My Mind reflects:
I agree Soul voice. This journey offers such fulfillment and joy that the thought of venturing forward without awareness to the assistance available and with knowledge of our chosen mission is not a thought I choose to entertain.

**Rejoice in the joy of life—
and the task of each growth step—
... The Angels of The Light.**

Chapter Twelve:

Insight from the Heavens

Energy—Light—Colour

Section I: What are Angels?

Event: Itinerary glimpse from The Angels of The Light:
You are given answers to your questions—insight and description of the Angels—what the Angels do for you—and guiding quotes to inspire the clarity of your path?

My Mind lifts to further insight:
I'm thrilled to share the insights received over years from The Angels of The Light. I must thank you, Soul, for your assistance in simplifying this wisdom to enhance my understanding—helping me *to get a grip*, so to speak.

My Soul replies:
My pleasure, it has been quite the journey and more fun times await!

My Mind opens to more information:
As this sharing of insight within this book is offered for inspiration, the following response was received

Insight from the Heavens

to my query to The Angels of The Light, to fully describe who and what they are.

❖ What are Angels?

We are Energy—we are Light—we are Colour—we are the essence and vibrations of The ALL—we are the substance of the heavens to the seeing of ALL and to this the directions are given as to the workings of the universe—we are the giving of ALL as directed from The Source—we are to give of The ALL/The Source of ALL ... The Angels of The Light.

My Soul adds:
My light is the all sustaining energy of The ALL Source. As the Angels are the vibrations of The ALL Source, we differ in this way. Our team is sustained in the Energy, Light and Colour of this ALL Source. Open your grasp of this my travelling companion.

My Mind absorbs:
So our Angels help us to switch on the light in our mind, body and ego *(our team)*. Our Soul retains its Colour, its Energy, and its Light within us and our team is supported with these energies as well. *Such powerful and empowering visual and tangible thoughts!*

Energy—this appears to also be all around us as well as within us. The dictionary defines Energy as: *an inherent power to produce an effect, vigour, or expression.* My thoughts on energy take me to visualize the heated air from above a flame or the liquid air energy lifting off the hot sun baked pavement. A magnetic friction with a strong gravity pull like a magnet has invisible energy and static friction energy can become charged between clothing. The wind offers us a warm or cool breeze on the skin that appears to be energy. The somewhat invisible aura surrounding humans, pets, nature, and other objects also displays a moving liquid-air energy.

    I have come to realize a trained focus on two of our six senses—*Vision and Touch*—will enable this lifted awareness to embrace energy in our daily lives.

- **The Angels of The Light comment on Energy:**

Energy—it is of a source within and without—the approach to life and the lift to see—we are in and of this field of energy ... The Angels of The Light.

My Mind reflects:
LIGHT—light appears all around us in our aura or energy field as well as within us as the colour of my soul. These I have witnessed personally. The dictionary interprets light as: *a form of radiant energy, illuminating and having little gravity.*

- **The Angels of The Light comment on Light:**

We help to switch on the light in your Mind—Ego—and—Body—the Soul does maintain this light within its energies—we highlight and lift your inner knowing of energy with guidance to choices of best—your gift of choice remains constant whether you follow the illuminated path or not—the love of The ALL Source offers a continuous highlighted path—the focus is to the open knowing of love and to this we

address as it is in this area of such that we continue to move—and turn on the lights within your team ... The Angels of The Light.

- ❖ **The Angels of The Light offer insight on Colour:**

Colour is a life force of many moving energies ... The Angels of The Light.

My Mind responds and recalls:
I am gaining understanding of these energies. The Colour of Angels' wings were so beautifully iridescent and radiant and I felt the energy of a euphoric love during my visit to heaven. An amazing vision of this light and colour within me was recognized one night in a huge cough. My energies were spent while recovery from a cold. I had retired early to bed. *Then it happened in the darkened room. At the start of this cough, I was sitting up and quickly fell back from the exertion. Surprisingly, I witnessed an astounding trail of light and colour seeming to explode out of my mouth. It was a stream of golden light that engaged my vision during this explosive cough. Is this an inner energy aura field?* I will definitely have to ask my Soul about this amazing colour-stream of light. I had a vision of your brilliant golden aura, Soul. What do you say now?

My Soul responds:
It is a miracle! Just joking, you have come a long way, girl! Yes, I maintain my energy in this golden vibrant colour. More understanding is offered to you as we venture onward. There is more energy, light and colour fun on the horizon!

My Mind gains further insight:
Colour—the shades of colour are limitless as apparent within our earth family appearance. The dictionary defines Colour as: *light that splits into different speed frequencies, wavelengths of energy that appear to the eye in the object they absorb.*

    Wow, colour is also defined in speed frequencies as well as energies that we see as the object the colour is absorbed within. This sure expands my observation of those thousands of colour paint chips presented for decor selection. This gives me a wonderful visual of your colour wavelength of energy, as well my Soul.

The Angels of The Light comment:
We delight in bringing colourful messages to your vision lens—we attract your attention to a vibrant rainbow—a colourful ball of light—a glowing flower or a vision within your mind's eye.

My Soul adds:
The rainbow shape and colours offer you a glimpse of how the human aura can appear, as you now know, Gloria. The human aura is an energy field surrounding our form. It is the shaping or suspension of atoms and molecules framing this body form that I, as the Soul, reside within. It consists of colours of energy, and is seen in layers, or shades of intensity, waves, blotches or circles. It is a visual acceptance that you, my Mind friend, can alter what you see, by altering how you see it here.

❖ **What is the Angels' task with us?**

We share the All Source energies—light and

colour with you—we are the vibrations of The ALL—expand this vision to embrace the infinite—energy—light and colour of heavenly guidance—we are assigned the task of assistance and guidance in all areas of your life—we also give freely our eternal love—as it is to this focus of All *(God/Creator)* direction—we shower upon you this unconditional acceptance to your tasks of choice—as the love flows and our focus remains—it is to this focus of ALL and the expression to gain—we do assist—guide and direct in your best interest always—you are truly loved … The Angels of The Light.

Section 2: Questions—Questions—Questions:

My Mind notes: I continue to have many questions! I am sure you do too! It is healthy to be inquisitive, is the encouragement I receive from my Soul. Soul, I have questions here on our journey as part of this team. Very anxious to hear your answers and welcome insight from the Angels.

Questions from others, as well as some of my own follow here. You may recognize the ones you have always wanted to ask. These questions were presented during meditations and the responses follow here from The Angels of The Light via automatic writings.

My Soul guides:
Listen to your truth bell as it rings in your Mind, my friend. This will engage a personal heightened intuition and connection with me as we choose action for our forward movement together.

The Angels of The Light comment:
Angel awareness is the rebirthing of your knowing and the observation of the seemingly invisible.

- **What name do you use to refer to God?**

Response: The name we use to refer to God is—The ALL—The Source of ALL.

- **What size do you appear to us?**

Response: We appear to you in a size of the smallest of the small to the largest of the large—in minuscule and huge—as we see the need—it is the presentation of each situation—of impact or attention of the message we deliver.

- **Is there a specific emotional time that you appear to us?**

Response: We appear to you all the time—you are mostly unaware of this—as the visual ability is not in focus. As for a specific emotional time—it comes clear to us when you need us most—and when you are in focus of your adventure there—we do come to you whenever you reach to us.

- **How do we know if you're a good Angel?**

Response: We are of love and light—our words are of this and the warmth is felt—we touch your love deep within and embrace you in same without.

❖ **Are there bad Angels, the dark side?**

Response: We do answer this here—the dark side exists for those who do choose this—as it is to this they give energy—we say—that what you accept as truth you give energy to—we do not put an emphasis on this as the way of life is to be in love and light—we do say it is of the gift of choice here to choose—of which you choose to place energy—we do not give any energy to manifesting of dark focus.

❖ **If we do not give energy to the dark side, are we to become oblivious to the possible existence of it?**

Response: We say here—the placing of energies is what feed the thought—and as it is to the choice of selection the attention is to be noted—the power to manifest is attached to the growth of energies—we do assist you always—you have only to focus on the light of love.

❖ **How would you describe the difference between humans and yourselves, in emotions, sensations, and senses?**

Response: We see the difference as—abilities of perception—as it is less obvious or acute to you to observe and hear the intricate and the volume of sound of this universe—as for emotions—senses—and sensations—we are also of these—and to the magnitude that exceeds your present abilities—it is to be compared as the abilities and knowing of a child—to the abilities and knowing of

a wise sage—to cite an example—some of the knowing is there—however—application and know how is undeveloped—we are of the knowing of ALL and this continuous ever-changing process—we do reach out and sense your senses and respond in the best of the whole—which includes you—as we move you into this all knowing.

❖ Why are you in this invisible state in the heavens and we are here on earth?

Response: As it is set up—the magic of this universe is in many unfolding wonders—continuously—we are in the place of choice—as you are—and there are reasons for everything.

❖ Do you need shelter or rest as we do?

Response: We only need the expanse of our work—it is of no shelter—as the energies—light—and colour are interwoven and of a continuous movement—we do not need an overprotection of this sort—as we are of the ALL source and of this we are directed—the energy is never ending and therefore need of rest is unnecessary.

❖ How do you know when we need help?

Response: We are always in tune—as you would say—it is to this we respond—the assistance is all part of or a coordination of the ALL plan and workings of your universe—we do respond always as you request and to this you are not always aware—we hear your every request—as it is directed to the ALL.

❖ **How can you be everywhere in an instant?**

Response: As we have the ability of movement—to a degree yet unknown to you—we do not need the lapse of time to move into one place or to another—therefore—we are wherever and everywhere as the example of thought ignites—and then quicker—we are an interconnecting overview of the wonder of the ALL—thereby—enabling a grid overview if you will—and also a non-confinement of this grid—it is of an absorption of ALL.

❖ **Do Angels ever pass away? If so, where do you go?**

Response: We are of an energy source and therefore do not cease—the change or rebirth is to offer here a glimpse of this process as the soul is encased in form—and this form does exhaust itself—the soul moves on—we do also—however—we do not need the soul form for encasement—we are of a continuous energy source and of a movement of such—as it is to the desires and direction of ALL—we do continue this assistance of creation in many ways and therefore—do expand with these directions—we are always there—in continuous and changing functions—we do not leave to go anywhere as we are in the ALL—of the ALL.

❖ **Do you have a guideline as to when you**

can intervene, in our best interest, to protect us from harm?

Response: We are in observation always—and we do reach out to you—the guideline—if any required—is the asking and then letting go to receive the protection from harm—as interwoven with your free choice—we do assist always to protect your interest of best—when you are in a fog of awareness—it is directed according to best—that the assistance is given to intervene—for the good of ALL.

❖ Can humans become Angels when they pass on? If so, in what capacity?

Response: We say here—this process of transformation to Angels is only of an illusion of inability—you hold now—the movement to release the soul enclosure or form is the process of lifting again to the energies of the ALL—we say here—there is one and the same in the universe—as the workings unfold—you are of soul and also of energy as the answer to your question is—yes—also you have choice to remain or move on to the direction of choice—and the capacity of the intricate working of the ALL—as the energies of the Angels—as the energies of the souls—as the infinite guides and more—all within and of the ALL source.

❖ What happens when humans pass over? Where do we go?

Response: You are lifted to view and observe—as it is to the growth gain—you are shown and encouraged to again choose—and place yourself of soul into energies of the universal grid—you are given love—eternal—total and unconditional—and the process begins anew—you go to the place of choice and selection of same—as it is to the offering of the ALL.

❖ Can Angels live among us on earth? If so, for how long and for what reason?

Response: We do and for many reasons—the length of time—as you see it—differs and the degree of involvement is set—we do assist you in many ways—many venues—this can be to stimulate—growth—change—insight—awareness—observation—love—desires—engage movement—and many other tasks—as it is best—of the ALL.

❖ Do Angels help with our dreams? If so, in what way?

Response: We do assist here—as it is to choice of observation—the messages are given continuously as in observation of direction of best—we do offer a guidance in this area of communication as well as others—the receiver of the message is open in the dream state—however—recall and understanding of these messages is in the choice of the individual soul—it is wise to request of self to the observation of these dream messages and their application to the direction of self is the key here—it is always to self-growth the guide.

- ❖ How do you receive direction from Creator?

Response: We are of the Creator's energies—and thereby do have a constant link—this is of an always open receiver—the example of an overall receipt of the direction and pulse of the wind.

- ❖ How many Angels does each human have?

Response: You have access to ALL *(God/Creator)* and therefore the multitudes are available—we are to say also here—you are given the constant guidance of The ALL—and the selection of at least three of these Angel vibrations of The ALL—the movement does however remain continuous and therefore changeable.

- ❖ Do our Guardian Angels stay with us for our lifetime here or forever?

Response: Yes, we are to increase and decrease during the growth—of the soul.

- ❖ Do you take our soul traveling in our sleep? Also in astral traveling?

Response: It is of delight for us to engage in this exercise of insight to the soul growth—we do assist—yes—in the travel of observation—as the soul does develop to this level of choice.

- ❖ Do you care about money?

Response: The power placed on the money of desire—is in most instances misplaced—we do assist in this knowing and as the placement is corrected to the overall gain in energy—to the avenue of growth it provides—the power of need is replaced to the power of continuous flow—we do say here—the choice of placement of this knowing is of assistance—or not—to each of you—as the awareness and grasp of the energy flow of this universe is observed—we place no specific importance on the power of money as it is powerless in itself—without the clear observation of the flow of energies—and the abundance of same.

❖ Is there a special way to talk to an Angel?

Response: There is a very special way—and that is to open the self to love—we do reach you in all your attempts and in all available avenues you have become aware of—the approach of love however does reach and open a huge connection—and engage the flow of our energies as these are offered to lift your insight of the ALL.

❖ Do the numbers of one's Angels increase as you get older?

Response: As it is mentioned here before—the multitude of Angels are available always—and as the soul expands in growth the access to this heavenly assistance is broadened—it is offered to each soul—at the growth of this soul—and not necessarily the age of the form—as this may differ—in the growth of insight.

❖ **Why don't you give us an absolute visual sign or vision, rather than making us figure it out?**

Response: What would be the fun of that—we do humour here—we do give you absolute visual signs—and also encourage the growth of thought—it is the desire of observation coupled with the trust of the ALL—and the movement to this trust—that does engage an open observation of our assistance—and signs of vision in the absolute.

❖ **Are all religions part of God's soul groups, each having a piece of the puzzle to complete the whole?**

Response: We answer here—the structure of religion is of itself and the soul groups are of themselves—each of desires and each of intent—we do say—the gift of observation does overlap as it does in the flow of ALL—as it is in religion the structure is of beginning and end—and the beginning of soul is of no end—but a continuous movement in the flow of ALL—as it is fair here to say the intent and desire of religion is to be praised—however—the structure does interfere with the movement to the flow of ALL—the pieces of the puzzle are offered within and without structured groups of religion—therefore offered to all individual souls—the growth is individual and the sharing is encouraged of this insight—the message of the universe is of observation of best when one is lifted above the restraints *(Closed thoughts. Lift above the stand of knowing it all, to see a universal message.)* of any absolute knowing—the groups are of energies of the heavens and of guidance of the intricate combination of thoughts to lift the whole.

❖ If judgment, competition, and ego were removed from religious organization, would movement into love based on understanding and acceptance of freedom for all be obvious?

Response: We do see this as helpful—as assistance to the lift to observe—the desire to grow and encourage this growth of soul in love is the best approach—the removal of these three mentioned desires of power—can assist however somewhat misdirected—the changing of these desires to the positive power of—observation—acceptance—and love—is the better choice—as everything is exactly as the results of choices taken—the unfolding of the universe is the focus recommended—and the observation of each soul's place in this unfolding is the choice of the soul—the movement to love is the only way to place oneself into gratitude and observation of same—giving way to visual and inner knowing of the workings of the ALL.

❖ Why do we have a veil of forgetfulness in life?

Response: It is a chosen selection and the need to assist a movement forward to the adventure of seeking the light—if you are consciously aware of the answers before you put yourself into the course of study—then the challenge of the exercise is then removed—remember you can choose this adventure—for the pure joy of soul growth—allow yourself to move into full enjoyment of the expression and observation—with insight of the life you chose.

- ❖ **How do our precious departed children move on? How are they taken care of?**

Response: We say here the need to move on is of a strong desire and one we encourage—the move is to a joy of being—and it is assisted by many—the move is to a lift of knowing and a journey of insight—the path is guided and assisted always—we do place an embrace of heavenly love upon these souls and do move with them—the way of choice is given to them and the selection is theirs—there is a task for each of them in the gentle love of the ALL—we do assist and expand their knowing—it is to the movement forward they are directed and their selections are numerous in choice—we do say here—the movement of these souls is of a high priority and of a gentle love—as it is to them an open path—we also assist on each and every step—the concern is of no need as the souls of these children are embraced in—total—eternal—and unconditional love—they are blessed.

❖ **Do you socialize with each other by writing poetry, making music, dancing, discussing problems, bonding, and connecting as we do?**

Response: We do communicate with each other and do bond—the exercise of poetry—music—dance—etc. is of an undertaking in expression of some—as to the whole we do enjoy the expanse of these joys of heaven—it is to an open expression of knowing and an acceptance of ALL that the music—poetry and dance is embraced—we do have all of these and more within our energies—it is to this delight of being of movement and expression is engulfed—as for discussing problems—the role of an Angel is to assist always as guided by the source of ALL—we do engage in the bonding of knowing this—through the intermixing of our energies—we are of one and of the ALL.

❖ **Angels of The Light, will you comment please on the synchronistic life work of Lady Diana, Princess of Wales, and Mother Theresa. Were they Angels in disguise, with the focus to their work?**

Response: We begin here—the calling is to love—we do prepare here to release in a touch of the examples of such to assist many—it is to a warmth of such you are to expand—we do express the place of such is in a joy of ALL—we are in a position to reach the areas now of such need—Lady Diana and Mother Theresa were of an instructional mode as in example—the source is within as we embrace the path of love—we say yes they were Angels—Angels in disguise—as you put it—their accomplishment is shown around the world—we do express there are a multitude of these Angels on your soil and in your lives—we do express the need—to become alert to love and express same—it is to a talk in such we do engage as we prepare to write this book—as our soul reach is to the many there—we rejoice—it is in an example the path is set and assistance to others given there—on this we do explain—we are in position to engage with those who seek the path—these two as well as for others—as it is a loss in your reality of body there they are to linger in soul form and assist—as you are to receive there you can determine and express of yourself in your work by remaining in center—on this we embrace you—the clearing to self is in a look to the surface as of thoughts and to heed these thoughts—on this it is to be said an open soul is wise—as it is their work we do share it is also of their example we do prepare on this with love—to express on a view of earth the placement of these two souls received an acknowledgment and appreciation of such loving work—this is of genuine love and this we highlight—as it can continue to gain of love in ALL—we do give of these messages—the touch is to be of mighty power and as it is to queue the rest of the senses—the release of love is then offered to receive—we do express here further on this touch—we do open you to the awareness of ALL—the issues are in a looking to self first and then an open expression of love.

❖ Do we give ourselves clues to our life mission? If so, how and what?

Response: We do say here—the plan at pre-birth is of selection for you—as to enhance the growth and knowing of the soul—we say here you have a choice to place clues within your life plan—as you are aware of and agreeable to this forgetfulness you move into—as for clues of what kind—we list here a few—your name—as you bond with your parents and suggest this to them in love—also the selection of your parents—to set up the examples and skills you desire on your chosen path—the placing of signs of attention to the triple numbers—and certain numbers of significance—and also a taking to observation of the existence of inner energies at times of insight—as it is a long list here we do say you are very clever in your selections and it is thus a personal list for many—we do assist you in the highlighting of each of your chosen choices—the selection process is filled of anticipated joy and excitement of the adventure you undertake—it is to this joy it is wise to recall—and allow the sparkle within each soul to shine—we celebrate your every move to joy or accomplishment—large or small—and delight in your choice to accept our guidance in your lives ... The Angels of The Light.

❖ **God/The ALL, The Angels of The Light, please can you enlighten us as to what can be done on an individual basis, to enhance the coexistence of harmony and peace in our world?**

Response: We express here—it is of an open view to the seeking of one's soul needs that is a basic expression—it is to this awareness that an individual requires the nourishment of self-discovery in all aspects and the freedom to choose—a soul growth expansion that will encourage harmony and peace in your universe—on an individual vision—it is movement forward on each path chosen and the awareness of infinite choice gifted to all—and insightfully focused upon self—that offers the movement to the power of love and peace—the seeking—the searching—the awareness of this journey selected and the intention to focus on favourable interaction with other souls—is the step to highlight on each individual journey there—aware of the ease of application with each step forward—it is in celebration of The ALL Love you are held—look to self-discovery—listen to soul wisdom—and open to our guidance from the Source of ALL—blessings can be counted as observations lifted to assist the empowerment of the individual to be a collective soul in the masses—embrace one's own journey with the adventure of discovery—on the soul level—as the individual missions become part and completion of the whole—a big picture to a gain of momentum and to the start and gathering of insight—a wisdom of love is the application and awareness of the mission of the whole—the future is made of individual contribution in a growth to again recall this need of source expression in peace and harmony—as each soul there remains in the total—eternal—and unconditional love of The ALL Source—you are truly blessed—your Angels of The Light—The ALL.

❖ In addition to finding the somewhat hidden clues within our names, what are the most important self-discoveries for us to make here?

Response: There is a looking glass journey to take—as it will become reflective and lift your observation—to a gain of your empowerment on the journey there—we say here—the best approach is the insatiable searching of a full meaning to life—as to the most important self-discoveries—it is a view of self in the respect to your chosen birth date—this will give insight to your traits—when in balance or out of balance—as your ego interacts with your soul—also it is the steps forward to engage in a vision of your Overview Mission—this is your main intent—to accomplish with soul growth—the vision of self continues with a journey onto the opening of doors on your path—the trust in self and the connection to your soul voice—as it is wise to gain this balanced insight to your direction of best—the colour of your magnetic pull is of assistance to you—as it is the descriptive of each colour that impacts the awareness of your distinct and individual selection of comfort there—we do also suggest the opening of a refocus to see the seemingly perceived invisible colours and energies—it does enable the strengthening of The ALL connection and does also engage the confidence within and without—on this we do say—the most important discoveries are the reasons you chose this life journey—the reasons are again somewhat hidden—yet will appear to be displayed openly to you upon the discovery of same—the use of your imagery and visual thoughts does lift to you this awareness—the meditation of intent is of assistance—in this discovery—your journey is displayed in full living colour to you always—it is the rediscovery that does explain the reason for the journey choice and it is in this the adventure—awaits to recognition—lift to see your life plan—and facilitate this lifting by self-discovery—you are assisted always—engage our assistance—listen to your wise and ALL connecting soul voice—and enjoy the journey there—with a positive approach in all you encounter—this does then maintain your precious energy connection with The ALL Source.

❖ The Angels of The Light, can you please describe heaven fully to us?

Response: It is of a full engagement of The ALL Love—it is of spectacular beauty—it is in full colour—it is of a reception place of love—we will describe here—it is in a full engagement to the vision of ALL Love—it is of the magnificent colour of the rainbow—as it is offered here to you in the words of your understanding—we continue—it is of heaven we all engage the most powerful energy of love—it is in this engagement the visions of miracles are orchestrated—this is your proof of our assistance with you there on your journey of choice—the position of heaven is your favourite happy place—it is of all these visions and more—it is a continuous opportunity to engage further soul growth—it is in the containment of a near place in your universe—it is of a similar descriptive of a hologram to you within vision yet somewhat filled with hidden distant visions to engage a closer look—it is very close to you in the distance of your time frame—it is accessible—yes—in your meditations and astral travel trips and also dreams.

There are full and complete vista views—of nature with mountains—trees of all species—plus all the flora you now recognize and more—you are encouraged when visiting to explore and engage the spectacular beauty of heaven—it is your home—though you are now away from home—yet also remain close to home—there are magnificent architectural buildings and landscape marvels—it is always perfectly displayed and engaging to growth of wisdom—there is never-ending options and choices as a continuous menu of examination.

The inhabitants are the souls or ALL

energies and these are of groups placed in ALL knowing—advancement freedom of choice and the full energies of love—are within the base of this heavenly order—the inhabitants contain souls of all levels of insight—with baby souls—to the wise sage—the guiding souls on acceptance to assist individual souls on their heavenly path—as do we Angels—they remain attentive as this assistance we do focus on—offering insight of the journey chosen—and do also celebrate each gain of soul growth.

As to the levels of hierarchy we comment here—the engagement of soul energies in the growth and wisdom of each—does then place a lifting into sections of the whole—it is within each section that the term completion of growth holds a display of levels—within each section engagement of the focus of The ALL Love assistance exists—as for levels in responsibilities there are distinction by tasks—it is in this the engagement of ALL assimilates to a huge family with a strong family tie—yet uniquely different with individual focus—it is of a soul entity the heavens are layered and yet ALL engaged—it is of a separation only of choice—of desired growth—of direction of ALL—as of further understanding to inhabitants—we speak here of Soul Spirit Guides—Angels—Heavenly Family—as in all the Saints and Prophets—to which Jesus—Mother Mary—for example are included—in a seemingly immediate family label—yet not of a separation in any way—all are accessible—approachable—and open in a superior coexistence—the engagement of ALL Love does offer an open door approach with access encouraged.

It is of perfection in all ways—it is of total—eternal—and everlasting love—the ALL blessing engages in this place of heaven—we say it is near to you—in the descriptive approach—of being able to reach out and grasp—it is close to your earthly ability to visit—to return to—when your mission there is completed—and also it is the position of everywhere—as if a universal view from on high can offer—the vision of an aura space encompassing and encapsulating the universe—in all its expanse.

As you recall the aura is displayed in layers of colour—this is also an applied and embracing of ALL repetition in a clever way of offering souls this insight to the workings of ALL reflection—this reflection of repetition is placed on a large and small scale—throughout your universe—there is not difficulty or stress—and certainly not negativity in heaven—there is a full and openly encouraged embrace of growth to continue the higher vibration of ALL Source.

This explanation is only limited here—by words—and your understanding—we will offer further information individually—as one requests—and also in more detail—your grasp is now in filtering—and engaging of your soul voice—continue this path to illumination—you are held in the ALL Love—The Angels of The Light.

A Mirroring Discovery with Angel Visitation—Gloria Messenger

❖ **Is the Soul the same as the Spirit?**

Response: There is separation when on Earth School for—the Soul—Spirit Guide and Angels—when the Soul returns it is not noted as separation—only seen as a piece of the whole—the Soul is contained within the body—the Spirit Guide is an energy form of the heavens and not contained—as are the Angels—the Spirit and Soul are seen as separate on the earth plane because of the separation of place—and when the Soul returns—the coming together of the whole reunites these pieces of ALL Source.

❖ **Does God get upset when we talk to Angels first? We are never to worship any other than God, it is said!**

Response: We are the vibrations of God—the fingers if you will—it is of addressing a piece of the whole—it is of this analogy we give you—as a parent yourself—(and as God also is) should your children—(or the Angels) choose to address or show love to another member of the family—grandparents for example—(or you earthly souls) would you as the proud parent—(or God in this analogy) feel upset or threatened in any way(?)—no—God does not experience this threat when you talk to The Angels of The Light—as God is the source of ALL—there is nothing in the universe that is not part of the whole—your communication with us is encouraged.

My Mind exclaims:
Wow, Soul, can you believe this? Oh yes, I hear you saying, *I already knew it*. Well, I am feeling very uplifted with this insightful information. *Heaven on earth!* I wondered and now I have been given a glimpse of the truth within this phrase. The hologram example of the human aura encourages me to take liberty to thoughts of a parallel universe concept. That the proximity of heaven is very close; the thought of possible duplication or layering effect lifts to be examined; and we may have echoed a remembrance of heaven with our earthly world architecture and gardens. So intriguing! I think I am getting it now, Soul. We can choose to follow this illuminated path of insight or not. We can choose to experience this unconditional and eternal ALL love or not. Accessing our gift of free-will is a choice. Life takes on a whole new meaning as the journey of discovery continues. I am so grateful for this guidance from The ALL Source. My gratitude extends to you, Soul. I am so thankful that I listen for your voice.

Thoughts of my Mind come together:
Bringing it all together is an amazing insight for me of the past years of my acknowledged guidance with The Angels of The Light. There seems to be a reason for all my experiences that then lead into the recognized use of application for this new experience. Just like a gathering of research or, accessing the talents gained from previous jobs to apply to the present task. Each experience holds information or a previous memory of use that can be reapplied. Well Soul, you now know that I do not

mind at all delivering this message *to celebrate the joy of Angel Love!* Do I hear your soul voice?

My Soul expands:
I did not think you would mind, Mind, once you understood your chosen mission. I encourage your renewed vigour to take on this mission adventure with this knowing of the inspirational support available. To a fault of being repetitious here, *there is more to come—hold on and enjoy!*

Section 3: Levels of Growth:

Entry: Itinerary glimpse from The Angels of The Light:
You continue your journey there with a heightened awareness—this awareness enables you to begin to connect the dots or find the missing pieces to your puzzle of life—synchronicity is a new word of awe in your vocabulary—you embrace the vision of your perfect home.

My Mind visualizes:
There seems to be so much to learn and so little time to apply it! I do see how my life appears to be just falling into place, and obviously beyond co-incidence. Yes, I do love this word — synchronicity.

My Soul encourages:
It is all in Divine Order! Take your time to process and enjoy as you move forward.

My Mind is in relief:
Thanks, Soul voice. I needed that pat on the back to release my anxieties of retaining all this

important information and then to deliver it on this journey we share. So thrilled to know of our secured partnership.

- ❖ **Quote from The Angels of The Light— printed in first issue of the Angel Awareness newsletter—1996.**

Give to all you meet in the way of love and understanding—as it is only this awareness of connection to all and everything—that you grow and learn and remember what you didn't know you knew.

My Mind is thoughtful:
Okay, Soul, what was that you just said? Oh yes, I need a plan to apply my insights. Set up a databank in my mind to sort and retain all this. Possibly journal and write it down? I want to learn and remember what I didn't know I knew.

- ❖ **Quote from The Angels of The Light— printed in second issue of the Angel Awareness newsletter—1996.**

The best way to advance on your path is to become aware of your blocks *(hurts, regrets, and attitude)*—**thus you gain power of awareness to choose releasing these negative energies and begin focusing on your unique action of love—to assist to dissipate same.**

My Mind expresses:
I have many more questions. Are there any shortcuts, Soul?

My Soul responds:
The shortcuts to the ALL Love do not involve missing out on our growth events. To grasp the ALL Love at any point during this adventure with desire for illumination, is the key to receiving the truth that resonates with each soul. This applies to the position we retain at any given moment. We are moving forward quickly as we experience our chosen itinerary entries. With application of awareness during the event or in a review after the event has played out it is to be remembered, time is not a factor at these junctures to open to the ALL love insight. You could come to the realization of our chosen path at any time during the journey, my Mind companion.

❖ **Quote from The Angels of The Light—printed in fourth issue of Angel Awareness newsletter—1997.**

An open knowing is the key to insight and the vision of life—we assist as you request.

My Mind asks:
Soul, can you give me insight as to where I am now on my path?

My Soul explains the Levels of Growth. This may help you here. Observe the four levels of growth:

> ➤ **A Desire and Action level:** begins with the choice to connect. This is a desire to improve one's approach to life.
> ➤ **A Happiness High level:** is achieved when one chooses to live in daily gratitude and thankfulness. This level is achieved

with a lift of trust and action of giving thanks.
- ➢ **A Gathering level:** when momentum is being built to gain insight and knowledge of gifts. A desire to learn more with the action of meditation is engaged in this level.
- ➢ **A Destiny level:** when the wake-up call is heard and the mind encourages the ego to maintain balance. Desire to pray. To ask for divine assistance to enhanced action impact of achievement and approach to one's mission intention is the observation of this level.

Use wisely our gift of freedom to choose. I will offer continuous promptings to you of our choices of best, my Mind companion.

My Mind gains insight:
I very much appreciate the promptings of your voice, Soul. This intuitive inner voice echoes the words of guidance you offer. Okay, the level I appear to be at is Gathering Level and moving forward. This is good to observe the prior movement on my path.

My Soul encourages:
Now to keep moving *upward and onward!* —as the saying here is noted. Remember to enjoy the ease and lightness of each step, my Mind friend.

- ❖ **Quote from The Angels of The Light— printed in fifth issue of Angel Awareness newsletter—1997.**

If you are to reach understanding and visualize your truth—the process is in the awakened

state of intention to seek out—the road is unique to all as the twist and turns are of your choosing—we are always in position to assist—as you request.

Entry: Itinerary glimpse from The Angels of The Light:
You enjoy the feeling of lightness as you focus on purging excess material items—living with only the items used to enhance your goal of soul growth is your desire.

My Mind reflects:
New observation, even though I have plenty of storage now; I really do have a desire to keep it clear of items. No excess clutter. I recognize that my mind functions better with a clean and tidy area to work. Is that in preparation for more things to come?

My Soul emphasises:
Yes, it is also soul growth to free self of unnecessary material collections. This allows for a freedom of movement with room to expand insight.

My Mind comments:
Good, I do enjoy this clearing. Thanks for the encouragement.

Entry: Itinerary glimpse from The Angels of The Light:
You move to a temporary home—you are compelled to research genealogy—you compile a book of ancestry research—treasured photos—family trees—and trivia—just in time for a family reunion—this book celebrates your earth family—your husband

recovers from a serious illness—three years later you move into your dream home.

My Mind expands:
I like the fit of these new digs. Just the right size for the two of us. Even though I have more storage now than ever before, I have no desire to fill it up. Interesting?

Entry: Itinerary glimpse from The Angels of The Light:
You experience a brief illness—you release body weight to maintain a healthier form—you are now aware of the importance of healthy balance in your life there—a self-sustaining focus is now clear to you.

My Mind gains focus:
Is this body purging? It is nice to have this weight release. *Did I really choose this approach in applied choices that would lead to growing gallstones?* My diet choices, you say? Must take this insight and focus on better food choices for my body.

My Soul encourages:
Yes, your good health is important to maintain on this journey—as your energies will be taxed.

My Mind requests:
Thanks, Soul. I will need your help to curb my sweet tooth. You have my permission to yell at me when I need to pass up the extra sweets.

My Soul complies:
Okay, you got it. The volume will be turned up with assistance offered as well to focus on another thought.

My Mind engages:
Divine guidance at work again? I am led to order a book off the internet describing the benefits of a selected food combination. This book improves my understanding of the digestive system and the need to help it out with choosing to eat protein or carbohydrate meals separately accompanied only with vegetables. Now I have a plan, just need to focus willpower to apply it.

Entry: Itinerary glimpse from The Angels of The Light:
You begin to tie together your gains and insight as you prepare to write a book—The Angels of The Light will guide you in this process—you are lifted with awe as the pages seem to fly in daily—ready to be typed into the book on computer screen—you truly count your blessings.

My Mind is excited:
This review of our growth together has been rewarding, don't you think, Soul? It is like we are sitting in an inner theater within my Mind watching a movie of ourselves *(our team)*. An inner sanctum! A safe place were amazing revelation is absorbed for understanding. *A true eye opener!*

My Soul is encouraged:
Yes, it does show growth on every page typed here. There is also more to celebrate ahead!

My Mind embraces:
Let us take it on together, hand in hand, now with my keen awareness of your assistance and existence.

My Soul inspires:
Oh, I would really like that! Good, here we go together then as Buzz Lightyear says—*To infinity and beyond!*

My Mind comments:
Guess I should buckle up to be prepared for more amazing adventures! Your use of these action phrases lead me to believe that you have been watching these cartoon movies with me and the grandchildren. But then you are a captive audience as I recall, you can only go where I go. Hmmm ... what movies do you want to watch next, my Soul companion?

Section 4: The ALL Love:

Expression of Love—Me and My Shadow

❖ **Quote from The Angels of The Light—printed in third issue of Angel Awareness newsletter—1996.**

Ask for an Angel Hug to touch you—request and send these Angel Hugs on to others—we have an abundance of love to share with you—ask and trust to receive ... The Angels of The Light.

The Angels of The Light share this ALL love: We are in the view of your every desire to seek understanding—we are with you in each step of awareness and we are with you on the intention to action—it is in ALL love you are moved forward—we do engage in all aspects of your journey there—it is the reach within

that dictates a length of step without—we do offer here this vision—it is like a stone is moved to show the home of an insect and the working of this insect's movements to survival that was hidden to you prior to moving the stone—now you are aware that there are workings in process somewhat hidden from your view—a parallel to be drawn to the universal continuum—we are in this vision you choose to explore and experience soul growth.

Examine the depth of this vision by turning over the stone—it is of explanation here to facilitate an awakening to the expanse of the ALL Source—we are of a continuous and an intricately detailed and orchestrated lifestyle—working in perfect harmony and based in love—just like your item number one—on your wish list for a dream job. *(First item on my list was a wish: To work for a large love-based company.)*

As to the full vision now we do say—it is only given here in a capsulation of each portion in order to express details—the capsule of love in ALL things and of ALL things—large or small—we do say to you the vision of a love that has no boundaries—it is a vastness with no endings and of a presence to fill and engage ALL beings—yes everything—this is the ALL love and the reach of this love is endless—beyond infinity as you say there.

ALL love that sustains and moves the direction taken by choice there—this love is of a description to engage miracles and it is to the observation to see ALL in the space of no time control—the carrying of love within does move the obstacles of mountains without—this is a vision of a hug of massive proportion—that never ends—and has no apparent beginnings to you—it has always been there—will always be there—and is ALL sustaining.

As we do engage your thoughts further—the expanse of love is of a depth and a height that gives to your overview of this universe you reside within—the path is a choice to explore and it is of this chosen path the turning and twisting—with the collection of wisdom gained—you drive the need to seek your answers and your own truth—it is of a full engaging rhythm of this ALL love the path clears and is presented to you with clarity—seeking to see is the first step you took—then the acceptance to action on your part engages momentum—as you reach out further now—we do offer to you this vision of ALL love—the expression is fuller than full—a solid knowing of being guided.

The colour is of brilliance as an enhanced vibration of light does reflect onto the whole of every colour—this offering a presentation of magnificence—as in our wings you observed during your visit.

On a look within this ALL love—we offer these thoughts of description—the carrying of the ladder to the skyscraper building and looking at the inability to gain the observation of climbing to the top of this skyscraper—with the inadequate length of your measure.

As to the sound of the ALL love—it is clarity of harmony to ALL orchestration—a multitude of Angels singing—or an innocent laugh from a baby—to everything in nature that engages a tone of ALL vibrations—with the recognition of pure joy and euphoric celebration.

There is also a smell to love—and it is in this you are drawn to journey there—it is of a scent that lingers gently and has staying power to lift and awaken the senses—the example here is of the smells of home that engage your relaxing—and the smells of freshness of nature on a dewy morning—these smells not only linger on your senses—they can trigger the memory and place your mind into the smell of love—ALL love.

Can you taste love? That is a question to explore here—as a piece of chocolate melts on the taste buds—it is said to be a taste of love—for some—the true taste of love is when you are not anticipating a pleasant taste—and the lift of your senses is engaged in a surprise to your mind—as it is unrecognizable as any taste you have ever experienced to food of any kind there—it is an indescribable taste of the engagement of ALL love.

And the intuitive love we offer here is of a guiding of the senses to an open door that voices your inner knowing—an engaging of your soul and hearing its guiding voice of wisdom of truth and of clarity.

Yes—you see we have used the gifts of your

six senses to describe the ALL love to you—feeling the touch of love—seeing the vision and expanse of love—smelling the fragrance of love—tasting the explosiveness of love—and also hearing the music of love—plus your intuitive knowing of love.

We access these six senses—as we alert you to the presence of ALL love—we are the vibrations of this complete—eternal—unconditional and everlasting ALL love you are surrounded within and of forever.

It is the—hallelujah of awareness—when you recognize the assistance always available to you.

This love is offered to every soul—entity—angel—spirit—saint—prophet—family of The All—which includes the male and female aspects—plus all other organisms of plant or animal—as it encompasses everything in the never-ending expanse of ALL Source and does join all together in harmony of intricate dance of love.

The magnificence of this—big picture of love—is the glimpse of The Source of ALL—in one aspect. We will continue further our explanation of other sections—to the volume that exists—for now absorb this—we will engage again tomorrow.

My Mind is overflowing in celebration:
(Hallelujah—this is a Hebrew word ... hallelu or praise; yăh or Jehovah.) It is this song Hallelujah by Canadian composer Leonard Cohen that has recently embraced my emotions. Canadian songstress K.D. Lang performed a soul-engaging version of this

love song of praise, at the 2010 Winter Olympics Opening Ceremony, held in Vancouver, British Columbia, Canada. I have taken to humming this melody when I want to connect with The ALL in a loving thank you; when I am preparing to handle any stress that may be coming my way; or when I am driving in my car without music present. The ALL love within this song must be what I feel. It puts me in a space of calm. *Could this calm space be a mirroring to the magical peace of the Heavens?*

With receiving of these automatic writings from The Angels of The Light, my skills acquired as a secretary/administrator are coming in handy. I wonder what other skills that I have gleaned while on this earth journey will be applied in the future. Oh, yes, I hear your voice, Soul. Patience will reveal it all! I am wondering how more pages of insight will fill this book. The stone has just been turned over to repeat the prior example given by The Angels.

The Angels say— Love is presented to us within our gifted Six Senses.

My Mind absorbs:
How easy is that, if we only have to become alert to the sense being accessed? A bigger picture of love with The ALL in everything we do, even the small things could be magical. When sitting hours in meditation/communication with The ALL/The Angels of The Light, my body can become stiff. However, my sense of touch is thoroughly being soothed in this wonderful treatment of a vibrating back cushion. Thanks, Terri, my treasured friend

your synchronistic gift is enhancing my work and preserves my team energies. *Could this small treat be expressed as a gift of love being Angel guided to fulfill my needs?* It does seem to align with the meaning of my middle name, and I do love spa treatments.

My Mind expresses:
The information in this book compiles many years of receiving words of wisdom, often given to me in the middle of the night. The urgent need to write down the words filling my head often disturbs my husband's sleep and I am thankful for his understanding of my work with The Angels of The Light. The recollection of my last thought before floating off to sleep one evening was a heightened appreciation of how lucky I am to have such a feeling of inner peace and gratitude of the love around me.

Expression of Love:

**The feeling of the word Love—
is quite remarkable and touching.**

**Take a moment to place one's self in—
the embrace of Angel love—
visualize walking into this love—
as if walking into a hug from your Angels.**

**Once engulfed in an embrace that is
total acceptance and unconditional—
allow your inner knowing to surface.**

**Stop for a while—soaking up this love—
aware of the movement through your body.**

**This heavenly embrace from God—
our heavenly parent—The ALL—
who gave us Angels—
to delight over us and guide
in our best interest—
available to us anytime we
wish to receive this love.**

**Give yourself permission to see and feel
this energizing enlightening love—
... The Angels of The Light**

My Mind enjoys:
Receiving these words of love does lift me into the space of Oneness! It offers me a glimpse of this Omni presence! The power of love can never be overstated.

My Mind inquires:
The All/The Angels of The Light, is there something you would like to add, change, or edit to the book up to here? I wrote out this question to start my meditation today.

The Angels of The Light respond:
It is in good order now—after you put in the Shadow poem—we give you more to add here—the work of reaching out to others as a messenger has been rewarding with the Angel portraits and messages—it is a wonderful confirmation to you when you see the acceptance the recipients of these portraits show by their creativity in including the Angels in their lives—from framing or laminating the portraits—by choosing special

coloured matting—by scanning and putting on their social media to share with others—by transferring onto a keychain—a bookmark—by creating their own letterhead—and also transferring their Angel portraits onto T-shirts—sweatshirts—handbags—the most unique so far has been to have their Angel portrait tattooed on their shoulder—now that is carrying their Angels always close.

Feb. 17, 2000—Received in a dream and woke to write down this poem from The Angels of The Light.
My SHADOW and ME!

Does it mimic my ego?
As a friend or foe?
Can it really tell me which way to go?

It mimics my every move.
Can it change my mood?

Playful at my will—
turning peering back at me.
Does it know?
Does it see?

It is a connected part of me?
As the wings to a bee—
it does not lift—or fly me away.
It does not work to enhance my day.

What can my shadow be—
but only a reflection of me—
movement of me?

A Mirroring Discovery with Angel Visitation—Gloria Messenger

But can it see—
what I want to be?

I can dance and sing—
and wave my arms.
I can play or stay—
turn quiet and still.

My shadow responds—
to my every will.

This shadow is fun.
This shadow is true.
This shadow does see—
the soul in me.

How can I display—
the lightness and joy?
The place I want to be—
where memories are free—
to lift and soar—
and hold me back no more.

Can I turn to my shadow—
look deep into its shading—
turn it over and around—
as if a gingerbread man?

I look to acknowledge.
A moment to share.

Never dragged down with stuff.
My shadow is whole.
My shadow is part.

Insight from the Heavens

It plays on any surface—
as a portrait of art.

Wherever I go—
I need not feed it—
though it can shrink and grow.

How I act—
what I say—
no emotion does it display.

This reflection of me—
it follows — it leads.
It disappears and returns—
hides under me.

The clothes I wear—
it does not care.
The selection to be—
is up to me—
in this time we share.

Can it show?
Can it lead?
Give direction to me?

Turn and look—
and say follow me?

The view is two of me—
turning — moving.
My shadow is always—
a part of me.

A Mirroring Discovery with Angel Visitation—Gloria Messenger

My shadow is playful.
It can make me smile.
If only I hesitate a moment—
to play in each mile.

How do I choose?
To present me to me?
Turning and twisting—
and trying to see—
a copy of me?

Add some sunlight—
noting this reflection to me.

Even as it is fading—
it holds on to my shape.
Its reflection is engaging—
and touches my soul.

A hug - an embrace.
Can I spare a moment?
To reflect in this space?
This body and soul reflection?

The call is deep—
as the shade of my shadow.
Can it wake my deep sleep?
so I may reap what I sow?

The intent — the choice
the focus — the embrace.
Does my shadow have a face?

Insight from the Heavens

I turn to see—
the view is new.
The selection is mine—
and can be divine.

Is it alive?
This refection of me?

So lightly it glides—
no surface too rough.
Is that how it guides?
Sometimes in front?
Sometimes behind?

Can it walk beside me?
And be my friend?
Can it turn to speak to me?
When I'm at wits end?

It feels no pain.
Does it reflect my gain?
Or display my loss—
with no material cost?

Is its sole purpose?
Just to play with me?

My shadow and me—
are one with thee.

My Mind opens:
I may have still retained a level of sleep while receiving this poem in automatic writing. The thoughts I recall are an acceptance to comply,

and that the writings were very fast. It was difficult to keep up with the flow of words. I returned to bed and fell quickly into a deep sleep. Amazement settled in when I woke in the morning to read these channelled barely legible scribblings. The lengthy writings in a poem form from the Angels of The Light have now propelled me into further awe of this adventure of spiritual growth.

Is my shadow an entity in its own right, popping up into view at opportune times to remind us to play in this life adventure? I do remember the giggling fun with grandchildren trying to dance with our shadows. *My shadow and me are one with thee—could this be that we truly are? A part of The ALL Source in shadow form? Are the Angels playing in our shadow with us?* They can appear in any shape or form to alert our attention! *Are they engaging our mirror reflection at these times, ready and able to resurface when the time is right, wherever there is light?* Well, now I want to play with my shadow and expand these thoughts of its illusive display.

Entry: Itinerary glimpse from The Angels of The Light:
Your husband will have important involvement on your future soul growth itinerary—he will be a trusted companion to you.

My Soul informs:
He will enjoy the travel and fun. Pay attention to his needs as he is a big part of our journey. Do not leave him unattended.

My Mind is surprised:
Really?

My Soul replies:
Just putting it out there.

My Mind accepts:
Okay, thanks for the heads up, Soul.

Section 5—Abundant Choices:

Entry: Itinerary glimpse from The Angels of The Light:
In the vision of The ALL—now you will reach out more—this vision that sustains you also engages your need for more information.

My Mind requests:
Yes, please give me more insight. It fills me with reassurance of the thought that my journey here is not haphazard. There really is a reason for everything!

The Angels write:
The meditation compact disc we facilitated through you has helped in many ways as it also reaches out—you have been told of how a rambunctious puppy immediately settled down and sat in front of the stereo speaker—not moving until the CD stopped playing—recently you were told of a family of dogs who became alert from their slumber when the CD began to play—they sat at attention—looked around and moved closer to the sound and began to stare at their owner—our voices have a profound effect on people—as you personally know—and now you are aware of how we also connect with pets and animals—also sharing the energies of The ALL Source.

Entry: Itinerary glimpse from The Angels of The Light:
You have recognized the—reason—season—forever soul friendships engaging your journey there—you have a renewed energy to understand the reasons why such role-playing was necessary on your chosen path—you also come to recognize that this role-playing is each soul's choice in accepting this casting call—for the interactive assistance and lessons you are both to receive as your soul growth itineraries criss-cross.

My Mind reflects:
Moving forward without some friendships held together does put me into reflection here. The reason, the season, the forever souls and the lessons offered to me. They all take time to absorb and very sad when friendships end. Life here does not appear to offer shortcuts, only exit ramps and detours. *Is this all a mirroring effect too?*

My Soul answers:
You will gain clarity in the need for this soon. You must just soldier on for now.

My Mind accepts this reassurance:
Okay, Soul voice, as long as you remain close.

Entry: Itinerary glimpse from The Angels of The Light:
You now embark on a twelve-year path of continuous growth—these events appear to be startlingly different from what went before—you are awakening to bigger opportunities than you ever consciously dreamt of.

My Mind expresses:
Who knew?

My Soul engages:
I did!

My Mind requests:
Oh yes, you know it all, Soul. Any hints?

My Soul offers:
Humongous changes ahead—remember to say thanks!

My Mind imagines:
So exciting!

A) **Visual Thought of The ALL and Angel Connection:**

The Angels of The Light write:
We do say here—the work is progressing nicely—we are in the vision of ALL now and do offer to you the magnitude of this vision—it is of a glow—a source—an energy—an illumination—a reflection of all colours—and also a solidifying of space—we are of The ALL and it is to this visual the connection is encouraged—take the first step into this place of ALL love with the forming of this visual thought—the journey ahead is to engage this energy thought in all you approach as if you are always entertained by Angels—we are *(as Angels and the vibrations of ALL)* with you always and are the embrace your soul desires to fully engage the growth of your future path—as you carry this thought vision with you—it is of a look to self and an observation

of the path that is highlighted to you—the carrying outward of your mission does assist and offer the inspiration to others to engage their paths in more clarity—seek to add this thought in all you do—we are engaged with you.

B) Gaining the Big Picture of our Soul Journey Preparations:

As The ALL wisdom continues—it is of the big picture we offer—your future path is in a taking off position—the colours and light also display our energies to you—it is noted that the carrying on of your momentum can assist in the process to implement a secondary path—and in this way your soul growth is emphasized.

C) A Secondary Path—Shadow Path:

This path is a Shadow Path—it does assist others and encourages their leaps forward—as you look within it is of a voice you recognize as your Soul that is heard—we do assist this volume lift to partner your walk together in joy on the path—we say this to you—in the anticipated perception of assistance to others—the shadow path is of a heightened awareness and does parallel the soul journey as it becomes apparent to you—we are to continue here—the path of a shadow is in the choice of pre-birth and is in addition to enhance your original soul growth intent—it is of a singular attempt to emphasize the learning and accelerate the lessons—this shadow path is engaged only when the soul growth has grown to a level of acceptance to The ALL Source—and the divine timing does then present the emphasis to task there—you choose a complementary intent for your shadow path and this intent is of enhancing to the original—the focus is in a positive and productive—a rendering of the big picture—to engage in ALL knowing—it is in this choice you are determined to grow illuminated to solidify your gained insight.

As it is of a choice to addition of this shadow path—you also are offered the intricate mapping out of the direction taken—it is a big helping of Joy you include and a total engaging of soul connection—it is the application of talents gleaned along your path that lift to you now—the view is contained and we do shelter you with this acceptance—adventures of joy continue as you embrace this shadow path—and the walk is of a pace you desire—it is of lightness and ease and fills you in the Joy of ALL.

Every soul does have the opportunity to select a shadow path—it is of an additional emphasis to the original intent to soul growth—and is of need to engage further focus as in The ALL gift of free will—it is entirely a choice of each soul as the pre-birth itinerary is completed—should the soul not complete this additional path of parallel—it is then offered the observation of review in the debriefing process upon arrival here—and the gains are noted in part or whole.

It is to the multitudes of choices we do speak of now and expand also on the Shadow Path—the choices are endless and are ever changing in the desire to create a unique adventure on one's soul path—the choices are unique to you as they are unique to each and every other soul—this does then allow the fine-tuning desired to initiate a perfect path to achievement.

The choices are of—a huge helping of positive loving—energizing—and lifting inner knowing to enable an enhanced possibility to complete success—the options are—also of seeking to carry lesser loads—it is of this option that the predesigned path—will benefit of a reduced challenge and events written in your itinerary—the option is included for the benefit of an addendum of choice or an escape clause—so to speak—if this option is accessed during a struggle to fulfill an event on your itinerary—and there shows a definite detour offered to the soul—the clarity of your options and choices remains totally within the soul—and is voiced at times of perceived application—yes you are given a Shadow Path to choose to place a parallel emphasis on your original itinerary—and along with this additional path—you have the choice of adding to the impact of the growth—or at any time lessening the impact of the growth—as the soul chooses—all is choreographed by the soul in the dance of your life there—and is assisted by divine timing of The ALL Source.

D) The Choice of Gifts:

We do remain always near to assist your clarity of these choices and others—we will expand on this here—as we say there are abundant choices offered and selected when compiling your itinerary—there is the choice of gifts—these are the gifts of The ALL—and do place an ease of approach and ability to engage the activities in a display of talents on your path—the ease to you is gifted in the same unique attention to detail that is maintained in the full preparation and selections on your itinerary—it is of this enabling to succeed on the Soul growth that is the focus of the ALL Source to embrace you within and of the infinity of unconditional love.

Choices are of selection and observation as to the choice of best in application to the desired outcome—you are always and forever held within the safety of The ALL Love and given the insight needed to enable the choices of best—it is of clarity all choices are made prior to the Soul's engaging within this form chosen—on the adventure you set out to achieve success in completion—to the highest level also selected—yes—you also choose the level of achievement—and set the bar at your own choosing in height of success.

My Mind absorbs:

The compartment of soul-growth-knowing within this brain is showing expansion of space to enable the retention of this insight. Files are set up with subtitles of choices that are to observe my traits, character comfort, and a life approach with the needed tools or talents for success. It is all in a colour coded display and surrounded by the awareness of ALL Love within our six senses, engaging self-motivation, as well as a reflection to self. *Now I have a Shadow Path file tab. Joy*! This word has always been a desire for me to achieve and maintain. Interesting now that it is used to remind me of one of my chosen tools or pre-set focuses for achieving success? A shadow path of Joy is a wonderfully engaging thought. I love this choice, Soul.

My Soul replies:
Yes, the choices seem endless, and they are! You are recognizing how Joy is a goal for our soul growth. The gifts of abilities have been set up to access, as well as how the Angels assist us as they access our six senses to alert their messages. Now you see that we have an escape plan, should we desire to access it. Now, how is that not being prepared? Stay open—the insights continue for you to absorb, my Mind friend. More Joy waits!

My Mind recalls:
Escape Clause: My understanding of this term is from my real estate career. It can be interpreted to mean an option included for the protection of the purchaser to engage the opportunity to end an agreement should the written details not have been met to the complete satisfaction of the purchaser. Now it applies to my itinerary! Any further comment on this escape option, Soul?

My Soul explains:
You have the concept with the above; it is a backup

plan and used only in the circumstances of the movement of growth being denied by the choice of another Soul. Should this be seen as the best choice of action, this option is selected with a glimpse to the outcome.

E) Multiple and Group Choices:

The Angels of The Light continue:
It is clear to the Soul the need to prepare and select all possible situations or probable situations that may or may not develop during your journey there—as it is on the journey you chose that you retain free will to continue selection during your pre-set or aborted events.

We do say here the choices are also in multiples and are also grouped in each scenario the purpose of this grouping is to assist a clear thought process during your earth adventure—we continue here—the choices also contained in application to the selection of your parents for example—this then leads to the selection of your genes and appearance there as well as the character-building experiences with probable and all variables of choices of free will accessed by your parents.

We move on to guardians now and explain the need to be adopted or raised by another soul—other than your parents—this is also a probable prearranged path of possibility—when this path of being raised by another soul—other than parents is taken—then a selection of choices are available to access

during this switch of route—you will then choose to experience another set of choices before you return to the main path of awareness to soul mission intention—this is like the journey you experience here—on earth as you gain in the tools and talents needed to express fully your mission choice—in the work experiences the talents perfected and the traits of personality—awareness to these choices are offered at early age there—until you return home here.

Therefore—again it is wise to connect with your Soul and access the guiding wisdom to facilitate choices of best—to remain on the soul growth intended path—this is not to say that there cannot be growth gained when a detour is taken—it is very much included in the overall growth and can also assist your application to mission—however—it will be experienced in difficulty and will not play out in ease—during the gathering of this detour growth.

As you design every aspect of your chosen mission expression—you also select and arrange the interaction of other souls on your path—this enables the heightened opportunities to lesson growth you choose to gather—this does fit well with your understanding of friends for a reason—as season—and a lifetime—as you engage fully with the expression of a loving approach to all interaction with other souls there—you will also gain the insight and the illumination of path—an access to the ease of movement as

the synchronicities become openly displayed to you *(our pre-planned itinerary includes lessons to learn via other souls. This is mutually agreed upon role playing. When we maintain a loving approach of interaction, the lesson becomes clearer for soul growth.)*

The continuous flow of ALL Love is your power tool to access. No—not in an electrical or battery-operated power tool—even if you do have *Tim the tool man Taylor* to enhance the power torque there—just a bit of release there to the weight of this information. *(attempt to stay light in this loving approach)*

My Mind reflects:
This information was flying in, and it did appear to be heavy with insight. Overwhelmed with doubts of my ability to present and grasp this insight, I internalized that the readers may feel the same. The next day, I was physically exhausted with no apparent reason until you enlightened me, Soul. Choosing to hang on to this feeling led to the recognition that my body had to deal with this anxiety. I immediately asked the Angels to help me absorb this insightful information in ease. Then when transcribing these insightful writings, it became clear that the Angels had placed the insights in sections with headings to assist clarity—something I had missed during my stress.

My Soul ensures:
Eyes and ears open now to proceed without worry! Just take your time to absorb, my Mind friend.

F) Why do you Choose Illness?

The Angels of The Light continue:
We are to offer you a lightness of thought here—you do plan out your itinerary in an anticipated excitement to a wonderful adventure—you are aware during this selection process that you will have emotions to deal with on your earthly journey—that you do not experience as you reside in the space of heaven—other than love—this can be paralleled somewhat with your experience of pain—yes—it is not experienced in heaven—when a mother gives birth or you heal from a surgery or an injury you experience pain—yet once you fully recover or see your miracle of birth baby—you have a vague remembrance of the pain you endured.

As to why you experience these roller-coaster emotions or the impact of pain—we express here—you choose these additional aspects of your journey to assist the heightening of your awareness—to make corrections—or put yourself back on track—and also to fulfill a contract to offer another example here—to become a mother for another soul.

It is of a seeking with each and every step—each and every thought or concept—you choose to select during your journey of choice—that engages the opportunity to lift yourself into the awareness of The ALL Love—we do offer another analogy to this seeking—the taking on of this soul growth adventure—you evolve into a higher vibration soul or entity here in heaven—and it is your

intent to succeed in your selected focus—as you on earth do desire to improve your status in life or succeed in completion of a project—the overview is also placed in your itinerary and this event prearranged by you does engage a lift to the option again remaining always with you—to access your lifting of the veil of forgetfulness—with a glimpse of the big picture—we are to assist you on your chosen path always and we do celebrate with you these times of insight—no cakes or balloons in sight but a full-on Angel chorus of jubilation is expressed outward into the heavens—the expanse of this wondrous music does then signal to others here that a big picture insight or giant leap of faith—has occurred on earth—and this leads to a round of applause in heaven—so to describe it to you.

So in this visual you see how each and every soul on an earthly journey can make a difference—or make a mark—as they venture onward to success of their individual missions—it is not ever missed to offer a celebratory pat on your back—as you move into a lifting to see clearer your designed itinerary and soul growth mission.

G) The Work is Never Done until it is Done:

The expression—the work is never done until it is done—was a revelation at the time it was spoken there—as it gave the push in momentum that was required during the times of toiling in the fields of agriculture there—

this phrase still applies to all aspects of your journey—however—we remind you here—that the work does not require the difficulty of placing self in the acceptance to toil away in heavy backbreaking labour—unless that is your choice accessed there—all choices offer an ease of application and a difficulty of application—when you lift yourself to access your soul voice—you will see clearly the choices in this application—as you select—the pace out of each choice is set in motion—you can become alert to how the choice plays out—and select another approach—and then possibly choose the application to task of ease—your growth is not determined by the achievement in ease or difficulty—only that the application to a successful result in the completion.

As you asked prior here—do you pile it on—and say give me more—when developing your itinerary of soul growth—we do answer that question—yes—you do select to achieve a multitude of events to assist this growth—however you are given the choice of how you will approach each event whether it be in ease or difficulty—as you have also prepared the possibility of the difficult choice to unfold—as well as the approach of ease.

My Mind speaks:
Angels, you have written to me previously, always suggesting that I approach a task in ease, allowing the path to present synchronistic displays of the choice of best. I now have a renewed intention to

Insight from the Heavens

listen to the promptings of my soul, so I enjoy the ease of this divine guidance. Thank you!

The Angels respond:
You're welcome—we do celebrate this insight—and yes the chorus of Angels voices are echoing throughout heaven—you have more impact here than you realized—each soul's movement into insight is celebrated.

My Mind exclaims:
Soul, did you hear? We are celebrated with chorus of Angels as we achieve growth together here.

My Soul shares:
Yes, it is so very encouraging and motivating to know of this celebration of success.

**H) Seeking Clarity—
to Lift the Veil of Forgetfulness:**

The Angels of The Light continue:
We continue here to offer more insight—seeking to see clearly is a step into lifting the veil of forgetfulness—yes—as each soul lifts—a wave or expanse of this insight is felt there among all souls—this lift can facilitate a shift in the approach to your life path and is measured by the expression—a quantum leap—or a magnetic pull—that can enable others to accept this insight being presented—it can also be called a huge growth-enabling tool—or a momentum shift—this enables mankind there to facilitate movement to the next level of insight.

Now we speak of the levels of insight as before given to you—we do expand here—

the levels offer a measure and the reaching of each level presents an accomplishment to that aspect of the soul growth you have selected—we say further here—the continuous momentum is encouraged as we assist you there to remain on path—it is the full completion as example—each step up the ladder that enables your solidity of who you really are—what your inner soul voice expresses—and a move into the next chapter—as the page turns to offer another section of selected choices on your itinerary—that your soul voice expresses outward to you.

As this next chapter and the next chapter continue to be presented—the emotions offer to you an observation in a more even keel—so to say—the emotions present a solidity of step and therefore—more self-assured movement within your steps forward—we do also offer to you the gain received from the feelings of accomplishment—as well as the heightened intuition that engages you to begin to access these two of your six senses—*(intuition and touch)* on a high level of insight as well.

There are signs to your soul growth progress always available for you to observe—as you are in position to access a quicker pace—if you choose this application—you will notice that your life seems to have flown by in a review and your desire to capsulate it into photo albums and books is a clue there to you of this engagement of momentum chosen—it is to a suggestion we give here—to celebrate your achievements at every level—as do we—

allow yourself to celebrate and listen for the party that takes place here in heaven—in your honour—remember you are never alone there on your selected path chosen—to become aware of this assistance offered to you from The Source of ALL.

I) **Further Assistance!**—
   Twelve Areas of Further Assistance
   from the Source of ALL:

We talk here of further assistance—we are to describe here the placement of choice within the character of the soul experience there—it is in this selection that your disposition and your approach to life is prepared with always the option of choice remaining to engage otherwise—the character of the soul growth is a development of reaction and action to the events selected in your life.

   a. Choice of Character—Self-Preservation Option and Self-Motivation Focus.

We are with a mirror here—we hold with reflection given to you—note the reaction you take when cornered—or pressed to appease—or comply with the manipulation—or corralling approach from others—this reaction is set up as your Self-Preservation Option—in your case, Gloria—you withdraw and this is your need to preserve your energies—as you need this in place to balance your Self-Motivating Focus—you also choose in life—this keeps you in balance—if you choose to confront—as your self-preservation option—then your self-motivation focus would be misunderstood—and you would be out of balance on your path—and challenge would be seen as your lifestyle.

My Mind confirms:
Yes, I do see this as a fit to me. I do withdraw to avoid unnecessary conflict. Now I see how this chosen reaction of withdrawal does preserve my energies. It becomes an action when chosen with intent to formulate a positive approach. It also offers me the space of a moment in time to reconnect with my self-motivating focus, and make a choice of action.

The Angels of The Light comment:
There is a fit to all options and focuses on your pre-arranged path—these are complementary when accessed in the positive—and destructive when free will is accessed in the negative.

My Mind questions:
I see now how quickly I become off balance, especially with those close to me. Why is that, Angels?

The Angels of The Light explain:
You are holding high expectation of those close to you—to understand your needs—and this is a merry-go-round to give an example—because they also hold high expectations for you to be alert to their needs.
    You can observe this reaction to reaction—when displayed and played out—as it is continuous on your path there—however to enable a change into positive growth—you can

prepare self with thought to protecting your energies in self-preservation—and offering your excess energies outward in a form of gifts.

To offer an example here—balance self by an attention to the needs of your body of rest—exercise—and nourishment to sustain your energies—this then places you in the focus to self-preservation—and a renewed pride of this attention to looking after yourself—when you neglect this maintenance—your body is out of balance—and your form is therefore in low energy to perform in positive balance—in balance you can remain in a position of observer and open to your soul voice of guidance—out of balance you become closed and negative—emotions filter through to engage reaction decisions—the step to insight in this area of focus and option is a maintaining of the energies required to feed your self-motivation of momentum forward—and thereby remain open.

My Soul confirms:
Do you hear, my Mind friend, our balance means getting exercise, feeding this body well, and relaxing in laughter, with routine rest to maintain our energies.

My Mind responds:
Thanks for this motivational interjection, Soul. Glad to hear your voice is still driving me forward. Thanks also to The Angels for this insightful solution to stay balanced.

b. Connecting with Other Souls:

The Angels of The Light continue:
We continue here—and you're welcome—we are to share here information on the choices of Connecting with Other Souls now—as you remember—other souls accept the position to play out in your life also enabling a choice of growth in their lives—so a win-win situation you could say.

When the roles are played out as designed or scripted prior to birth—for each of you a benefit to both is the result—however when the souls choose to approach their part in another unscripted application to the lesson—a need to control—or dictate—or facilitate their change of plan—is the observation you will note—you can then choose to continue to play your part as if you say there—hitting your head against the wall—or up against irrational behaviour—and this perpetuates the repeat and repetition of the push to change the plan—opposing your Soul's desire to focus on playing out the original script—this usually is the reason for separation and divorce there—one of the partners has chosen to change the script agreed upon.

There are always ways to attempt an insight lift to the soul choosing the rewrite—however in most cases this is rejected—and a parting of ways occurs physically or emotionally or both—a need to open and observe these changes desired on the path of the re-writer is necessary—to return to original act in this play—you perform or agree upon a rewrite—

that embraces both souls to facilitate any forward movement—or an exit ramp is usually the choice—in this aspect of playing out the focus of another's growth.

Of consensual souls and also the application of this observation is with the reason person you mention in your life—the reason has been played out positively for actual mutual soul growth—or negative separation is the result and that is played out as a no win for either soul.

(This soul may have chosen to re-write the role playing, thereby obscuring the lesson or reason they agreed to present to you. Then opposite results of positive soul growth intention could occur within the interaction of this friendship.)

A negative as well as the positive can offer soul growth—in a lesser degree—this however can add baggage—as you say—to carry with you in your subconscious mind—as your soul directs you to continue forward movement.
(Each soul has an accepted interactive role to play out in our lives. This can be played out positive or negative as free-will is every soul's gift.)

c. Side Ventures:

We do offer this further insight—a need to maintain self—is also of favourable assistance to the draw to self of Side Ventures of short positive growth—we describe here an example of a Side Venture—when you take a short trip that can enhance your path of growth or not—if you choose a Side Venture—it is mostly observed as a regrouping of your emotional

energies—a refill of your tank—or a mini vacation—if you will engage that thought.

A Side Venture consists of a short experience of hope—in the return of your insight—or an opportunity to engage a refocus on your path—moving on forward quickly—past the recent rewrite or separation—to the laid out plan.

This is of a need in self—as well as a desire to move over the bump in the road—a Side Venture is an opportunity to reengage—it is taken with this intent—however depending on your level placement or achievement at choice to Side Ventures—a positive or negative result may occur—should you want to shake it off—regroup and reinforce the opening to soul direction—a positive growth will result—if you chose the negative of vengefulness—then a negative path will open and the vacation could turn into a nightmare.

Again the choice is gifted to you—and the suggestion to use it wisely is reinforced continuously—in hopes you may open to hear.

d. A Swing Exchange/Venture:

We move on now to explaining a Swing Exchange—we continue here—the full picture is not complete without mentioning the Swing Venture choices—these choices are the options you set up to take a seemingly totally new adventure—or focus in life there—it is really a lifting to let go of the weight of the past—when an abundance of negative luggage has been gathered—and this allows a cleansing—or purging to occur.

To give an example—this Swing Exchange Venture option is a choice you see as no other choice available—and the need is strong to move forward—and start over on your path—it is an option to another or a better approach to success with your mission path—as predesigned—similar to taking a new road that you were previously unaware of and a desire to lift above your heavy load of stress—this Swing Exchange Venture is an option set up for you to access or exchange when your predesigned plan of probable outcome takes a turn in the negative application to the free-choice of other souls within your prearranged role-playing manuscript—with the focus on their parts to rewrite the first—second and third acts—your level of insight will determine which act you will choose to access your Swing Exchange Venture—or take an exit ramp—to facilitate this gifted choice of free will.

When a Swing Venture option is chosen—your soul opens another manuscript—to guide you forward with all the predesigned aspects of this new manuscript—offering another approach to success with your mission of soul growth—this will include the events of your agenda altered—or exchanged—to reflect the Swing Venture—it will have a new prearranged soul group to play out their agreed upon manuscript—and will have all the intricate details selected to assist this new approach on your adventure of soul growth.

My Mind engages:
Wow, Angels, we really do cross all the *T's* and dot all the *i's* on this path of soul growth adventure we chose! Amazing, we arrive with fabulous party planner skills or should I rephrase that to say— life-planning skills. Of course, the assistance and insight of heavenly guidance of this designed life plan cannot be overstated. Thank you for all the assistance offered.

The Angels comment:
You're welcome! Yes—you are very clever—and you left nothing out—nothing to chance—as your path is scripted to succeed—and you are gifted with an edit team here—to assist this fine-tuning—as well as The ALL observation— to enable your desire and intent of successful soul growth.

e. Choice of Full Action:

We continue here with the Choice of Full Action—in this choice you are given the assistance to achieve your mission focus with the assistance of clear heavenly engagement— this choice is made when clarity is reached at higher level of seeking and with this choice you will feel exhilarated upon your path— noting how life is falling into place for you— and synchronicity of this divine timing will become obvious to you daily—as your focus is maintained to your awareness of your chosen mission.

As the choice is usually made at the attainment of a higher level of clarity to your chosen path—it is also accessible when the

Soul voice comes in loud and clear—to let go and let God take over.

To give an example of this Full Action choice in play—visualize a mouse trapped in a maze and you *as the provider of this mouse*—**literally pick it up and place it on a new approach to successfully find its way to the food—or success in navigating the maze.**

My Mind comments:
Great example—I can see this choice clearly. I do sense a lifting from the Divine Guidance *(the provider)* to gain clarity. So it happens either when I let go of control of insurmountable challenges and let God take over, or when I have attained a higher level of clarity with understanding my Soul's mission choice for the journey here and a focus is maintained to awareness of this mission adventure. Angels, is there any other times this choice can be accessed?

The Angels of The Light reply:
The access of this choice to Full Action is restricted to those two scenarios.

f. Choice of Withdrawal Action:

However, now this brings us to explain the Choice of Withdrawal Action—when the choice is made to withdrawal—it is a time when an abort to the plan of soul growth is accessed—there are several levels within this Withdrawal Action choice and one is when an incomplete opportunity is observed—or predicted as imminent and the soul chooses

to place itself in this exit seat—and return home. *(When the fight to live is exhausted.)*

This choice is never taken lightly by the soul—and can be placed in a position of imminent demise—in the hands of another—or by the hands of its form or mind body—like in suicide.

When the soul realizes the mind-body has chosen suicide—the Withdrawal Choice is set up to exit this life and return home to only immediately begin work involved of pre-designing a new soul growth plan—and scheduling another reincarnation.

When a soul is put in the position of victim however—to assault of the body—as in murder there—this ejection seat is engaged to enable a safe landing here in heaven.

g. Time Out Call Choice to Reincarnation:

Yes—now we speak of Reincarnation—it is of choice always in the aspect of soul growth—there is a Time Out Call choice that can be accessed by the soul—and this is available always—this Time Out choice is encouraged when a previous incarnation was unsuccessful—or only partially successful—and could have been pre-empted by a choice other than the soul's.

This then offers a reflective time here—in the safe love of The ALL—refilling the soul energies—also this refuelling choice is accessed when the soul is undecided as to engage another reincarnation to earth—or to access other options of soul growth.

h. Other Options of Soul Growth:

There are endless choices as mentioned previously and these include residing here in heaven to assist other souls on their reincarnations—as well as facilitate soul growth in the manner of giving this heavenly loving assistance to others in many ways of empowering growth—or in the assistance to a fine-tuning of the growth achieved in a scanning or review of reincarnation—to any given selection of the soul—this includes an editing of reverse soul growth—and compiling a viewing of the positive and successful achievement made on each accessed reincarnation.

If the positive review is chosen—the soul can then select the level of success—and then make another choice to enhance this level while residing in heaven—this choice may result in an accelerated momentum—or a measured gain towards the growth of its soul.

We do assist in all aspects and details of clarity to each soul choice made with the lighting of clarity to each choice.

i. A Glimpse into the Teaching of the Need for Soul Growth:

Now we do offer you a glimpse into teaching of the need for soul growth—it is of a beginning without end that the Soul begins this journey of enlightenment—the beginning is of a birth of energy to embrace The ALL love—and as the energy of soul moves into stages of inquisitiveness—the opportunity is offered to receive answers in many ways—including reincarnation.

Well within the never-ending and all-consuming fulfilling level of heaven—the soul blossoms as you could describe it—and as this expanse of blossoming occurs—the soul desires for more insight—as this is gifted and ingrained as you will visualize here—a part of the makeup of the soul's DNA.

To offer an understanding there for you—the soul is a piece of The ALL Source—and is held within and contained of The ALL Source forever and ever—the soul does not demise or cease to exist—and with the ingrained desire to improve on its understanding or insight of the working of the ALL—schools of learning are in place to assist the growth of insight for each soul.

One of these schools is earth—and the reincarnations to earth are just an enrollment in school—to give you an example.

❖ Angels, are there other schools for soul growth?

The Angels of The Light answer:
Yes—there are many other schools—some on other planets in your solar system—and some schools are located outside your solar system—as well as several schools within heaven.

As the soul is encouraged to engage more insight—the options of school choices are highlighted and guidance to the choice of best is offered—this then offers a glimpse to you of the workings of heaven.

❖ Can you explain, Angels, why would we

choose to incarnate here on earth, as opposed to learning in heaven where ALL love resides?

The Angels of The Light respond:
Your choice is made after much gathering and assimilation of a perfect fit for your soul growth—you do look at all the choices—you do look at your desired outcome—and the best choice becomes apparent to you.

You have abundant choices on earth when reincarnating—and you do enjoy setting out your itinerary—to promote the best soul growth level you desire—it is as if planning an adventure to discover hidden treasures—and therefore it is wise to uncover the hidden insight you have placed within this life adventure there—to assist your desired soul growth insight.

You are excited to attempt each incarnation—and do intricately arrange in this uniquely personalized itinerary—every event possible—or probable outcome—and anticipated growth of insight.

You go into these incarnations with your eyes wide open—to coin a phrase for you grasp there—and also agree to forget these details to embrace and enjoy the adventure of rediscovering your soul voice once there and accessing its wisdom to give you a leg up—or clarity of your chosen path with the choices of best to engage success.

As to other schools—many do not require the predesigned itinerary—and the soul can choose to experience an unknown path to growth—a surprise adventure—or going in blindfolded without an itinerary incarnation—you could say there is a similar approach to earth incarnation with the agreed upon forgetfulness to your intricate itinerary—and we see this similarity as well—however the earth journey retains endless choices—where other schools are restricted in choice—for specific reasons of ALL Source loving protection to the Soul.

This does complete for now this glimpse into your gifted choices of soul growth intentions for earth incarnation schooling.

j. Retention of Your Souls' Growth:

We move on to offering you insight to the retention of your Souls' growth—it is of a seeking to lift your agreed upon forgetfulness that you move into this insight gain—and now your desire to retain this information does offer you a desire to access the memory—in a retention of these facts of ALL love.

The area we speak of is an area of retention—this is the full vision of desire to remember and this is available in the place of storage within the brain of your form—this is then a duplication or backup system to your soul wisdom—it is only a partial back up—as you call it—as the soul does retain full insight.

We say further here—as a prevention to forgetfulness—it is recommended to recall and repeat to self this insight—as if in a review—the gain to you is further grasp and an in depth retention—as it is of a journey there your focused intention—it is of a necessity to engage a direction map—so to say—this map is the guide to you as co-pilot or navigator—yes—or your GPS voice.

My Mind comments:
Global Positioning System … interesting!

The Angels of The Light offer:
As it is clear to the Soul which path is best at every intersection you reach—it is the desire on your part that is accelerated to move—we are to offer further here—a chain of events are the catalyst to observe when big gains are experienced by you—and this connecting to gather momentum is to assist the impact of your retention impact—the amazement of such grouping of events within a short expanse of your time frame there—is to enable the flow of insight to engage you in the waking up and the lifting of your veil of forgetfulness.

It is to this we offer example here—you are on vacation as it is a journey within the journey of incarnation—the waking up to the aspect of a bigger picture does engage your mind—this then enables the desire to push past the fog of beginning a new day—and as your desire for momentum is accessed—you then take steps forward to open the door and embrace this new insight within your mind.

The span of this action is determined by the engaging of a hold on your reaction—it is the reaction that hinders the action and causes doubt to linger or pause you into no action—however as you move into the phase of explorer of the access of this big picture or open door—you are welcomed to proceed and take up to the looking glass—as the curiosity then assists your discovery of insight you didn't know previously—that you already knew. *(Our doubts hold us back. Move past our fears into discovery and possibly re-discovery as in a déjà vu experience of being there before. You could move your life journey into wonderful discovery of self-reflection and empowerment.)*

This is a confirmation to you that you are being guided or directed by an expert navigator—your soul—your desire to move forward is engaged with a joy presented that fills your being—and this is a driving factor when paired up with your self-preservation—and enhanced together with your gifted self-motivator.

It is of clarity to engage in this big picture knowing that does then lead your adventure there—as it is of a journey to rejoin your original journey with the gain of soul growth—you do become more aware of this chosen adventure with each step forward—the carrying of heavy loads does not interest you—and your awareness is alerted to the guidance of your soul—as well as the ALL Source.

Take this observation into a vision of self-help—and add a huge helping of desire to enable the correct mix of insight to engage the ringing of your truth confirmation bell—this is the hearing of your wise soul voice—like a child looks to the parent for confirmation of a new bit of information given to them—this is your gauge to access your own pace and gathering insight—once you have taken the step to gather—to research—and to embrace the truth of these insights—the door remains open to your access as long as you desire to reach for and engage further insight.

As the gathering of this insightful knowledge is absorbed by the mind—it is then a signal to your Soul to move you yet again—to take another step into rediscovery—as you remember events of your past—it is of this identical storing of information you access to retain gathered insight—you just know you will remember—as you do a fond memory or a wonderful vacation.

These memories begin to fill you to the level as to delete the negative or the sad memories of discouraging times—and as you erase these non-treasured memories the empty space is filled with the adventure of discovering—with the memories of your renewed and joyful steps into the awareness of the ALL Source—a challenge may be what you anticipate for yourself—however when the access is retained and engaged in ease—the idea of a challenge dissolves into the excitement of the desire to gain more insight—we are in position always to assist—and as mentioned before we do enjoy the celebration of your forward movement.

My Mind accepts:
The Angel reminder messages have always been to approach challenges or soul growth with ease.

Synchronicity seems to put the right person in the right place to lead me to the results that I was seeking. It is this approach of ease that I have observed that appears to facilitate the movement. Do you wish to comment further, Soul?

My Soul responds:
Yes, the approach of ease is easier on me and you too. There are fewer obstacles on the path and a quicker achievement to the lesson for the growth observed.

My Mind engages:
I love this movement into joyful steps of awareness of The ALL Source, especially when the empty space created by deleting the negative memories is filled with positive adventures of discovery.

My Soul adds:
This lifting of insight into your retention, my Mind friend, is the beginning of great adventures to share. Onward to further clarity as I continue to navigate these steps that are assisted with the guidance from The Angels of The Light.

k. Trust within Self:

The Angels of The Light continue:
Now it is of a need to speak of the areas of trust within self—this is when the acceptance of your truth does reinforce your forward movement—your desire to engage the excitement of this movement does become exposed to the negative hits or cautions of other souls not at the parallel or advanced level.

As it is to self-preserve on your journey

there—it is also of importance to engage of the ALL Source love for added protection to your energies—as an example here—we offer this visual—the wrapping of yourself within the embrace of an Angel Hug does offer this protection to your emotional energies—it is within this embrace of ALL that our energies mix—and you do receive reinforcement to continue the momentum forward.

As an added example we say here—the look to the heavens is the looking up when the asking for help is desired—and this action of lifting your eyes and your mind does literally dump the thoughts of doubt from your mind—as this action is then placed in position to exempt a possible reaction to the perceived onset of emotional jabs—the jabber is then dissolved of the power to attack any verbal comment—that could have previously taken your energies of positive movement into the ALL love.

You do engage the strength to become independent to the good opinion of others—and you also gain awareness for their need to test your strength—and release their own doubts in the way of an open desire on their part to return you to the level they may be residing on—as it is of a journey of many levels—as previously mentioned—your stage of enlightenment is reinforced when you access the self-preservation of the Angel Hug and vision of The ALL Source love.

I. Abundant Blessings:

As it is in a momentum to offer this insight—we do say it is in blessings we now move to express here—the area of joy is a representation of blessings—this is an awareness gained to lift—to reinforce—and to express to self and others your excitement of this level you have attained—as you express this enlightened gain outward—the blessing of the ALL love sustains you—it embraces you—and it engages your desire to reconnect.

As you move into this gain of clarity—you also desire to embrace the emotion of gratitude—as it is of ALL love your path is activated—on the school of earth—you are offered this opportunity to explore—and to discover the hidden clues you prearranged to benefit your awareness lift—during this adventure of soul growth—it is in this opening to insight that you are lifted to see the abundance of blessings showered upon you—as gifted by the ALL Source.

The blessing of this journey to discover—or rediscover—you move into the gratitude and acceptance—as well as the lifted awareness of your gifts to assist your success during your journey on earth—as it is the mark of a lift into gratitude—the desire to express your heartfelt thanks is an expression you do engage in response to the awareness of these blessings bestowed upon you—an area of revelation to some souls to achieve your level of insight—does open the observations

to the magnitude of blessings in place for you to access on your path of soul growth.

As choices are never-ending—so are the gifting of blessings—as it is a closeness to the ALL Source you are engaging—the awareness of the magnitude of this eternal—unconditional—all sustaining source with Omni presence—does engage your awareness of this movement—into the blessings of assistance—of sustaining power—of your energy—of the intricately crafted journey you are on—of the joy within discovering your cleverly hidden clues—and also the blessings of soul connection.

It is to this lifted awareness of your blessings that your engagement to the acceleration of your journey—is brought to your attention—you are truly blessed—you are truly loved—you are never alone—you are gifted with all your needs to succeed on your predesigned soul growth path—with the blessings of The ALL Source.

My Mind expresses:
It is a space of expansiveness that I feel when expressing gratitude for the blessings in my life here. A space of infinite possibilities with opportunities presented for viewing. A feeling I can describe as total peace and secure grounding in preparation of the acceleration that waits to be engaged. I love being in this space and feeling so energized. Thank you again, Angels, for your vibrations from The ALL Source.

The Angels respond:
You're welcome! It is our task with you and the intention from The ALL Source to shower you within the ALL love as the blessings are gifted.

My Mind recalls a Dream *(Action or Reaction)*:

I had a dream last night that I was sewing shiny, dark blue, tiny seed beads in one-inch-wide letters onto the front of my husband's shirt. I was sewing these beads in a way to spell out these words: *We can maintain balance when we live in action rather than reaction*. Interesting how I am taking this insight into my dreams. Angels, do you have further insight to offer here?

The Angels say:
There is a replay of your events of the day when you dream—we do access your dreams in an area of review of the day's events—it is to this we highlight the gain of insight observed and replace the aspect of previous wonderings—in the adventures of the day it is in this you gain a continuous review of insight with noting of dreams we do carry forward the message gained to your observation.

It is the importance of this message of your dream that you are encouraged to absorb—because it was tediously and intentionally sewn onto the front of his shirt—another reminder if you will—of a thought-provoking tool—to access daily on your journey—it is also a suggested preparation—to keep your balance in the wake of reaction jabs of the near future—remember—we are here to protect you within our hugs—and your lift-up vision to the sky is encouraged.

My Mind requests:
Soul, can you add any further comments?

My Soul adds:
This dream is your desire to encourage your husband to gain understanding on his journey of

discovery as you offer him a guiding phrase to assist his movement forward. You are alerted now to his free choice. You are very aware now that you can only assist another soul—you cannot choose for them—or walk their path. Let go of this worry to his journey and let the hand of The ALL/God sustain you.

My Mind accepts:
Okay, let's stay close and open to each other as the choices of the future are displayed. I need the wisdom of your voice, my Soul companion.

My Soul quips:
Always here, can't go anywhere, you have me all to yourself.

My Mind is grateful:
Thanks, I need that reminder now. Love to see my next itinerary entry here. I must remain focused to continue my work with the Angels and complete this book.

J) Further Questions:

- ❖ **Angels of The Light, when light workers/healers see the forms or shapes of Spirits/Angels/Entities/Ghosts during their readings and healings, are they really seeing Angels? Please explain the type of being they are seeing. Thanks.**

The Angels explain:
These are in most cases—the soul entities of family that have passed on—and choose to visit there to assist a clarity or message—it is during these times of open communication that a message can be delivered.

   We as Angels appear mostly within an

aura of the earthy being however—we can also appear in other areas on earth—to offer assistance—or guidance—and also protection—we are in the realm of energy that does lift to heaven the entity spirit—and we are to assist their departure and re-entry to earth—as they choose—and as often as they choose—yes—we are like an Angel taxi—we do allow their presence to be acknowledged—and do not put our presence on view at that time—in most cases.

The impact of the entity's presence is the focus of the message—we assist all entity souls on their journey here and there—we are gifted to be in many places in the quickness of light.

A deceased member of one family is unable to become an Angel in the true sense—immediately—and unlikely to present to the healer or light worker other than as an entity soul—this soul recognition or description character is a comfort to the individual—and is consistent with the ALL love—it is only when one does not recognize the form as a family member deceased—that it is likely our presence is noted—the deceased entity is of assistance to us—as we are of assistance to them—a team of energies from the heavens—that assist to bring enlightened offerings of guidance to the forms of soul containment there on earth—it is the desire to assist your journey there—that we offer these sightings to you.

The carrying of light is our mission—and

we engage many ways or options to access the delivering of this ALL Love—we are of full colour—or lightness of movement—or quickness of energy—that is the preparation to engage—and alert you to a message of guidance—note when this is of observation—you will be more alert and aware of our existence with the desire to engage and lift your mind—it is in this way—we also assist your soul to lift your acknowledgment of its voice contained within you.

It is during these times—you are offered direction—to seek the ALL knowing of love—and lift yourself to engage this assistance—for example we offer here—the airmail message is given to you to observe and note—as it is of an importance to assist your choice of best—you check it out by listening to the voice of your best friend for authenticity or verification—your Soul voice—and before you act or move to address your choice of best—the awareness lifts to you—as to the best approach to take—this is the selection of the soul assistance that is encouraged on your path—we are of assistance also—as it is the Divine timing of ALL love we deliver—it is to this application or approach of best we assist—and your awareness is lifted ever so slightly—or in all the ranges of levels of openness to the ALL love awareness.

We are Angels—the entity is of a previous incarnation soul—as are the spirits that reside in heaven—the ghosts are souls who have not succeeded in the return to heaven—as of yet—

and in most cases their forms of energies are all that your awareness does engage there.

It is of an assistance always you are guided—in most cases—soul entities do not become Angels however—they do assist us—as we do them—as mentioned—we are of the vibrations of The ALL Source—were as the Soul Entity is of the energies of The ALL Source—the difference being—we are like the thoughts of The ALL—and Entity Souls are the desires of The ALL Source—for example—a thought is a process of engaging awareness to apply divine timing—a desire is the intention to gain in an action—this is of clarity as you reach to the next level of insight there.

❖ Angels of The Light, can you clarify for me the name meaning clues. Does the married name hold our desire to observer or experience the meaning within the name?

The Angels respond:
As it is the insight to all the names that offer clues to your mission—it is the married names you have chosen in pre-design of your itinerary—these names you accept to highlight to you—an experience—or a descriptive action—or a desire to maintain this trait within your mission approach.

Yes—these names will represent an observation of self-preservation and or self-motivation—they will also offer to you the traits and talents within—and a fulfillment to self to complete your impact and achievement to mission—it is in the insight gain—you examine—and then choose the next level of intention—an intention to proceed—or an intention to maintain the present level—until a self-motivating push is instigated by your soul—your ego—or your mind—we then highlight to you the path of best choice to accelerate your movement.

Your Overview Mission—as mentioned previously—is to offer to others the meaning of this overview display—you have selected only one—even though you possibly access several—to Share—to give Example—to Inspire—to Teach—to Heal.

Beginning with the overview mission word—then the first or given name meaning holds a description of your soul growth mission or purpose—the middle/nickname/baptismal names/etcetera—represent a focus placed on self in a look to self-preservation—the surname/adopted name/etcetera—represents the intent of directive to achievement or how to carry out the soul growth mission or purpose—the married name(s) then complete the somewhat hidden clues within the names—with the meaning within that surname offering a desired support or highlight to your path of proceeding on the best approach.

My Mind reviews:
It is a continuous amazement to me of the numerous clues placed within this life shared with my Soul. It is an exciting adventure to discover these clues with the prompting of my soul voice and gain clarity

of this path predesigned and chosen in every way. It is like fitting the pieces of a puzzle together with the guidance of someone who has previously put the puzzle together. I do really enjoy the assistance you offer, Soul, and truly welcome your prompting voice. Thank you!

My Soul adds:
It is close to the level of growth and insight soon that my voice will become louder to you and could also be heard as song. Just for a bit more fun on this journey we share!

K) Levels of Intention:

The Angels of The Light comment:
We continue here—the move into action is the engaging of a focused intent—the thought process is engaged at intervals—however the momentum of the action does carry the desired intent—the seeking to achieve—does also lift you to seek a lift into the next level of awareness—this is the support you need to prevent a slip into reaction where emotions are lifted and may cloud your perceived intention to attain your desire—it is the movement of action that you retain the power of the joy within each movement there—it is your satisfaction of achievement of your intended task that offers balance of self-team there on earth—we are with the move now to share your intention on the next level.

The seeking is the key and this seeking key unlocks for you awareness to a volume of intention—it is of the level you seek insight—that is the level given to you—we are of

guidance to you here—as in all aspects of your journey there your level of intention has been also predesigned to engage desire at the corresponding event on your itinerary.

As this event is carried out as prearranged—or changed in a swing venture for example—the corresponding intention is shifted to complement the desired choice and approach taken in reaction or action—if the choice is reactive to another's influence then the intention may be halted or derailed for a short time or longer—should the choice be activated in action to succeed then the intention level is illuminated to you and your success is guided to completion.

For example here—we say the taking of a short swing exchange venture is an intention to take a break from a stress situation—for a regrouping of your intentions—should your thoughts be engaged or distracted at this junction on your path of choices—then you may find yourself in a reaction approach to the plans presented by another soul—with a different intention than yours—if this is the case you can be shifted off your intention course and it may take you longer to return to your own path—you may choose to remain in the limbo of following another soul's path—however if you focus on your intention for a break from stress—with this swing venture—you maintain the focus to return soon to your own path—as the intention to your soul growth agenda is kept in full view to re-engage.

It is in this example you choose to take a

break and intend to return to focus—to self-motivation—as the break is completed—or to extend and again extend the break to the point where your original intention is forgotten or becomes a memory fog—this then describes the two levels of intention to action or reaction.

My Mind absorbs:
Action or reaction—it displays such an important and leading impact on the journey. Either of these choices inflicts a stalling or promoting of forward movement. The self-discovery of my probable reaction or possible action taken from an observation review of my past approaches is very insightful. When a forward movement choice is made with action, it must reinforce the journey, correct, Soul?

My Soul engages:
Yes, the choice of action is the vision of focused forward movement. This does indeed move us in the right direction. I will prompt your recognition for the need of forward movement. Together we focus to choices of action.

My Mind requests:
Okay, you lead the way when my mind becomes foggy during menopause.

My Soul offers:
No problem. Do you not recall that the eyes are the mirror to the Soul? I'll just shine my light on this mirror to navigate through the fog.

Insight from the Heavens

My Mind laughs:
You have the answer to everything. Just like you planned it out in detail!

My Soul opens further:
Yes, and am enjoying this open conversation with you, my Mind companion, as the path becomes even brighter for us. Our path is well lit, as The Angels say.

a. Intention Level to Hold Placement:

The Angels of The Light continue:
As we continue here—we give to you the intention level to hold placement—or to engage the movement to further insight.
   The example here—is that you can become content with the knowledge gained at this level—and choose to remain in the comfort of this level of ALL Love—this is a comfort zone for many souls—and does offer a certain protection zone to their gained awareness—the intention to engage the movement to further insight puts you back in the spaceship—so to say—as it is off to the unknown that your intention is guided—you may be excited yet apprehensive with this choice of intention because you do not recall the knowledge as yet of what you seek—and with facing the fear and taking on the journey anyway is a big push you give yourself.

My Mind reviews:
The four levels of intention—*Intention to Move into Action* with desired intent to achieve; *Intention to Move into Reaction* with intent halted on one's path

or illuminated to another soul's path; *Intention to Hold in Placement,* being satisfied with achieved insight gain; or *Intention to Engage the Movement to Further Insight.* Interestingly, there are so many insights you are giving here, Angels. I very much appreciate this glimpse into how to move along this chosen and predesigned itinerary journey. A team meeting for review on a regular basis could be helpful, do you agree Soul?

My Soul is playful:
Yes, you have your people contact my people to set up a time and place. Just joking here. We can meet at any moment you desire and in any place we are located! How is that for flexibility? And Angels, please know that you are always invited with your insightful wisdom and always facilitating our forward motivation. We are forever grateful.

The Angels of The Light respond:
You are again very welcome—it is our pleasure to highlight and illuminate these insights as we offer further guidance to all the incarnated souls there.

b. Level of Lightness and Joy:

The Angels of The Light continue:
As you see—we have addressed four levels of intention—there is one more level—and this is the level of Lightness and Joy—the intention level of Lightness and Joy is the engagement of The ALL love with the knowing of this engagement—and ALL Assistance is acknowledged—your soul voice is clearly heard and your ego is a positive partner

on your path as your mind remains open to the lightness and joy of this level—you are reconnected to The ALL love—and this reconnection is celebrated by your team there of Mind—Ego—Soul—Body as it is celebrated also by The Angels—and The ALL Source—Entities—and Family here.

When this level is reached in your intentions—your achievement to tasks is elevated and ease of accomplishment is anticipated with large strides in soul growth.

This Lightness and Joy Level of Intention does maintain your energies—and engage the move of enlightened choices to ease of success—on this level you make your mark—as predesigned—and move on your path with the confidence of ALL connection—you then choose your entries of itinerary with the awareness yourself (team) to the engagement of each—and the veil of forgetfulness appears non-existing at this stage or level.

As divine timing is highlighted to you—the choices made do attempt to coordinate with this heavenly rhythm—to facilitate the impact of your momentum of ability to success—it is at this level you enjoy the ability to chose and direct yourself on the path of Soul Growth—and with the ALL Connection—your gains are truly significant for yourself and others—the joy of this level of intention sustains you until you script otherwise—to return home.

L) The Carriage of Completion:

We now move into the Carriage of Completion—this is the final selection to your journey there—and it can be of the length of expanse of your choosing—or the time frame there that you choose in self-preservation.

It is in this carriage to close off the tasks at hand—and work to complete the tasks outstanding—it is an overview of your mission—and the review of the success achieved—as mentioned—this can be done quickly or in a pace of your desire.

The ride is engaged now—as it is the glean of awareness you and your team do take together on the finale of your journey of adventure there—when this step is reached in the lightness and joy level—you do openly know that it is time to say adieu and embrace the souls of those who remain there with the ALL love hugs.

If you are at another level of intention—this goodbye space is a less joyful or a surprise to grasp—and your need to embrace The ALL love is reinforced by the heavenly assistance to enable an ease of passage. *(When nearing the end of your days here possibly in a surprise illness and wanting more time to grow spiritually. You will still be assisted by your Angels even if you have not been open to them.)*

It is to the return you are greeted you are greeted with the full celebration of heaven and it is in this celebration—your level of intention is noted—reviewed and praised.

(Each soul is welcomed in heaven at every level of intention or stage of growth.)

As you are to prepare self to engage this level of intention—the glimpse of the joy and lightness you have been given—intrigues you and you are now in the pre-boarding stage of interest to learn more of the joy and lightness of this level of intention—the pre-boarding stage is a bit of a holding on to the need to apply a level of control to your tasks—as you become aware of this need to control the areas of your life there. *(As we are not privy to the exact time or day of our passing from earth. Realization is grasped at this point in the journey, that there is no time left to fix or open to spirituality in life.)*

Your choice to engage or not—this last level of joy and lightness with the intention to let go—and allow the magic of full-on synchronicity of divine timing to carry you onward and upward—as you say there. *(This is the last phase in our earth school journey. Know that our days are numbered in this phase and not allow fear to hold us back from achieving soul growth.)* **This is your insight for now ... The Angels of The Light.**

My Mind is ready:
My new focus is to action and my new level of focus intention is to joy and lightness. Angels, I greatly appreciate this insight and am eager to learn more. Soul, what is that I hear you say?

My Soul replies:
We have come a long way, girl. You have lifted with

intent to climb the levels of insight. Everything is in place to gain the security of insight on the level of joy and lightness. You're just going to love how the synchronicities play out and link together for us and others on our path. It is the home stretch for the length of time you have chosen to stay on this level. In your time frame, it is quite a number of years; in comparison to the divine timing—it is no-time. Enjoy the carriage ride!

M) **Colours of Lightness and Joy:**

We add here—the colours of lightness and joy are to be in a multitude of rainbow shades and expanding upon these shades in the vibrancy of each illumination of these colours.

It is to this we direct your attention—the full spectrum is offered in the visual display contained in the ALL vision—as you move forward into the insight within and of these colours—the answers to your questions lift with ease to the choice of best.

We reside within these colours as the vibrations of The ALL Source—it is of a genuine need to seek this vision—and it is displayed to you.

We say here further—the energies—lightness—and essence of The ALL lies within these colours for you to observe.

N) **Blending of Energies within Colours:**

We are of the colours—and within these colours of a magnificent rainbow—as mentioned and also the visual of a display of same does exist for you within as well as without—as you are

aware of in the energies within and without are available for all to see—within is the colour of your Soul's energy—and without is of the liquid air of your colourful aura.

It is in the mixing or blending of these energies within the colours—that enables your opening to the magnificent of The ALL love—and our unique connection—we are of this blending—as are you—we are of The ALL love—as are you—we are the vibrations of The ALL Love and you are the energies of The ALL Love—the desires and the intent—it is the awareness and the acceptance of the somewhat hidden energies and vibrations within the rainbow's colours—that is of assistance to lift your insight further—engage this visual—and enable your visual of The Source of ALL.

We say here further—the continuous display is given to you in the colour displayed within and without your Aura—it is of The ALL Source you are maintained there on earth—it is of this All love your journey is engaged—it is of the full vision we do assist—as you request—it is to this engagement of ALL your insight does expand into clarity of your chosen path.

As you engage this clarity—and enable your team of the Soul—Ego—Body—and the Mind—to enlist this assistance of the heavens—then you do open further the use and guiding assistance of this team effort to success of your intent—to engaging your mission in self- motivation and in the protection of your precious energies of The ALL love—in a self-preservation.

It is of the full spectrum of this vision of the magnificent colours of The ALL love—that propels forward movement for you now—to engage your team and remain open to the guidance from the heavens—the colours are filled with additional somewhat hidden clues for you.

My Mind exclaims:
Again I say, WOW! There is assistance placed everywhere on this journey and now within magnificent colours of liquid air of the human aura, as well as displayed in the magic of the rainbow. Angel energies engage in both of these outward displays of colour to lift our senses and capture our vision. Amazing and yet confirming my experience of viewing a brilliant golden colour of my Soul seeming to stream from within my body. Thank you for allowing me to view your empowering Soul colour! I wonder where else to uncover clues of colour on this adventure. Any advice, Soul Voice?

My Soul answers:
Well anytime, my Mind friend, you just have to listen. I will come to you in thoughts, in what has been described as that little voice in your head as I also access your inner knowing. Now you have also recognized the vision of my energy colour. Yes, our journey is assisted by Angel guidance, as well as the placement of these clever clues during the pre-design of this journey we take together. Though these clues remain somewhat hidden, my Mind friend, begin to open our senses further into

choices of colour. Acknowledge the existence of this additional help to the success of our mission. Your embrace of these discovered and accessed clues also lifts us into the level of joy and lightness, enabling further discoveries. Yes, there is more, and then more to see, to know, and to accept on this journey. It continues into a colourful, insightful adventure of The ALL love discovery or to describe it truthfully here, an ALL love rediscovery.

My Mind responds:
I am so glad to be part of our team, Soul, especially with you in the driver's seat. This Mind is listening closely to your wise assistance. I am excited to discover further somewhat hidden clues. Really have my eyes opened wide as I do not want to miss anything, especially colour of my choices!

O) Preparation to Gain Clarity:

The Angels of The Light continue:
We continue here—the path chosen is filled with clues of your placement—and it is enveloped or enclosed by The ALL Love assistance—this is offered to you as the blessings of The ALL Source—it is clear now to you—to prepare for and to open your desire to embrace the intent of awareness to The ALL Love.

As you prepare—it is suggested you take assistance from meditation—from exercise of the body and mind in the expanse of your breathing to engage your stamina—as example here—yoga—laughter—knowledge gained in books of synchronistic placement—focus to your attention—and in the maintenance of your body—in a balanced and nutritiously

individualized—to maintain and restore the form you inhabit—it is of these preparation steps you do engage the awareness of The ALL love—and open yourself to see clearly.

P) Sense of Self-Knowing:

It is to this self-knowing we address next here—it is in this area of security within that is the base and preparation to full vision—it is the full engagement of your soul placement and acknowledgment of its wisdom—with this awareness illuminated and accepted you begin to welcome this wise advice—and direction of best—and assemble your team—it is in the gain of clarity of knowing of your soul—that you then move yourself from the driver's seat—and welcome yourself to be Soul driven—on your predesigned journey there.

It is this decision to accept the position of observer of your path there—that the real strides begin to the growth of the soul—and as you accept the position of being along for the ride—you do also engage the pleasures of experiencing the shower of the gifts from The ALL Source.

Q) Observer—Twin Experience:

The position of observer is also a position of a twin experience—as this position is then shared with your ego—and does then set you up as twin observers—the awareness of your journey is then double fold—and displayed to be engaged in the mind as well as the

motivator of balance(*the ego*)—**this is the task your ego has signed up for—a journey of assistance to motivate your positive balance—and approach to this adventure—so as you gain this clarity—it is of the reinforcing—the intent of the ego—you assist to mirror or twin your design for successful soul growth.**

My Mind offers:
The ego is a twin to my mind? Twin observers—the ego and mind! I believe I owe my ego an apology! I previously considered it to be out to derail me from the positive approach to this journey, with a selfish focus of my energies. Now I understand that my ego is only reflecting or twinning with my mind, and vice-versa. I see now why it is so important to be aware of what thoughts my mind engages in, as these thoughts are also engaged by my ego. I now accept this discovery of a twin focus.

My Soul responds:
As the Mind, it is a task of pure sense of self-knowing you have accepted prior to the start of this journey. As it is clear to you now to access all tools all clues and all gifts of The ALL love, our success is thereby guaranteed. It is this task of importance we have taken on and the focus to self-discovery is our key to a hidden or somewhat hidden treasure. Glad to have you alert as an important player on our team Mind.

My Mind recalls:
My daughter and youngest sister have been part of a greeting card circulation with the phrase—*I was thinking of you—now you are thinking of me—ahhh the power of cards!* This phrase has been lifted to

me as a similar thought of my earth team. I am thinking of my Soul and Ego, and they are thinking of me (the Mind). *Ahhh—the power of the ALL Source! (My daughter and sister are both Gemini twin signs!)*

The Angels add:
Yes—it is in these small subtle yet powerful reminders you will lift to your awareness of the signs of guidance all around you—as it is a team effort on your journey there—your team is also assisted by the preselected players who execute their roles perfectly to assist your clarity and forward advance.

We are involved with the task to assist your team growth—by placing a desire to see yourself clearly—as if we place a mirror in front of you daily—it is not to have you focus on your looks and characteristics—other than to note them for the messages they offer you there—the more important reason for this mirror placement—is to enable a full self-knowing—as this is your motivating factor—and self-drive that assists you in the soul growth adventure—and also the dual position of the observer of this adventure—as you maintain the seats of ego and mind.

These appear to be lesser passenger seats—you will probably assume—however this would be the wrong assumption—as it is the presence and fine-tuned workings of both ego and mind—that enables and facilitates the ability to gain soul growth—without these three amigos in place—and moving forward as a team—obstacles and construction detours

will become the norm on your journey—as you venture forth there.

To enable and ensure a fun vacation journey with joy and lightness—your mutual agreement to acceptance of position—and focused intent is an absolute necessity.

R) A Positive Self-Absorption:

We now move on to inform you of the inclusion of a positive self-absorption. It is clearer to you now the need for the teamwork—and now it is important to maintain a positive self-absorption—to manage a balanced approach to this journey you have taken on.

The ego usually takes the hit for engaging the mind in a negative or self-absorbed approach to your journey—as it is blamed for having an agenda to control attention to self-absorption—however we remind you here of the twin seating—and also the position of the mind in this team.

The mind can also become filled with self-grandeur—filled with itself—with the desire to retain knowledge—in an insatiable display of trivia—or information that does block—or stack up as a library self-overflowing with distraction to the hidden encyclopaedias of wisdom pushed to the back of this mind-library—it is a note to self here to always place the ALL wisdom encyclopaedias to the forefront of your library—to enable quick access—it is to this intention you then initiate a clear awareness to your intentions of self-motivation—on a positive balance—as you gather other knowledge to assist your insight of The ALL Source.

We do say further here ... it is to a full picture of your journey there—that lifts your clarity—and illuminates your path filled with choices of best—the need to this self-acceptance of positive and desire for self-organization of mind—that enables the players on your team to perform in their highest degree of expression to The ALL Source awareness.

The candour of the team is an observation to celebrate—and as it is enabled to succeed in this attention to task—your gifts of humour—lightness—and joy do attach to the intent of this self-absorption of positive approach—and intent on your life adventure.

My Mind is inspired:
Reinforcement of my team positions with this visualization taken into meditation. This will definitely assist our team's intent to a positive self-absorption. So much amazing guidance offered!

S) Signs of Guided Wisdom:

The Angels of The Light continue:
Now it is a turn of the page in this book of insight that we offer you the signs of guided wisdom—we say here—we offer signs of guidance in many ways—we use your six senses extensively—and also we show our presence in times of stress or danger to assist you on your chosen path—also—we display these signs in the available technology you are in use of there—for example—we do appear to you in the sounds—as well as the visual—it

is a continuous loop we do bring the message and offer the answers of guidance to you—in a lyric of musical song—in the opposite of no sound—and also in the preparation to engage sound—as it is a choice of selection—we reach you in the action of reaction—and do also maintain an open vibrancy to all your daily occupation with your technology devices—as of yet—and will continue into the future.

We do also reach to you in action of the dance—the movement—the rhythm of the foot tapping—or the hand clapping—we celebrate with you—and rejoice as you lift to awareness on your path—it is in the engaging of this open awareness—that your lift into lightness and joy does engage awareness to our signs of guidance.

We do engage you in the awareness of a visual spectacular or magnificent view there on earth—this is to prepare your visual engagement of heavens wonders and brilliance of colour—we also engage your senses in the feel of the ALL love—in each refreshing drop of rain—and beginning dew of the day—it is in all this and more we reach out to offer assistance and guidance—we do alert all your senses—and embrace even your taste buds—to a surprise response of joy within your anticipated or non-anticipated intentions—it is of the smells of action that we move you—and also engage you to linger—it is this joy of life in ALL observation we lift to you—the desire to count your blessings—the abilities to task—we lift to you in ease of application—your intuitive knowings—that assist your cautions and heighten your quick reaction—is guided and enabled—we do open to you the floodgate of emotions—to lift to you the releasing cleanse that follows—it is in these areas we assist your thoughts of renewed awareness to the choices of best.

Your every step is highlighted to you on every selected path—it is in the looking up—and the selection of the thought of The ALL love that we do open to you the big picture—and clarity of The ALL love.

It is in joy we reach to assist your path of choice—and in lightness we offer assistance to your chosen journey there—as it is from The ALL Source we are guided—it is to you the empowerment of this return to clarity we do assist—now and forever—it is your gifted free will we attempt to engage—in a guidance to the awareness of The ALL Source—as it is with this awareness you do empower your soul growth into the vision of this ALL love—as this is engaged—the synchronicity of our guidance is illuminated to you—as it is a clarity of ALL that propels your journey into lightness and joy.

We do also assist your steps with empowerment—as you request this ALL love assistance. It is into a journey of light you are led—and your chosen mission is engaged in ease—we do assist to lift you to see—to hear—to smell—to taste—to feel—and to engage your intuitive knowings—you are held and showered with the brilliance of The ALL Love.

It is to a clarity you seek on your adventure of life there and it is a lifting we offer on each step you take—you have only to ask—to seek—to intend—to focus—and to engage the rhythm of this ALL love.

The journey of your choosing—and your choices taken—as well as your actions and reactions—do always remain in your ownership of free will—we desire to assist your clarity—and to offer to you the visions of ease of approach of best—to accompany your vacation there on earth—it is to the calm reflection of The All assistance that does offer this clarity—it is the embrace of your movement into awareness of The ALL Love that propels the speed of your forward Soul Growth.

We are of a closeness to you always—and do assist as you request—it is The ALL light you are offered illumination on your path of choice there—as you make adjustments to your journey—to engage this ALL embrace—you do open to the big picture and gain the awareness of your chosen mission with the tasks to attain further soul growth—we are ready—willing—and able to assist your clarity—it is and will remain your choice to lift to see The ALL love—the attempt of engagement to the ALL love is celebrated here—even in the smallest gain—it is in this visual your momentum to clarity is encouraged.

Rejoice with The ALL Source as you walk

within The ALL love—and lift your awareness to this empowering image—you are truly blessed—and encouraged as you begin this journey of soul growth—and will continue to be blessed and encouraged as you move into the awareness of this ALL assistance—as you are guided by your Guardian Angels of The Light—The ALL Light—and lifted into this ALL illumination.

My Mind expands:
Soul, this insight really ignites in me the desire to attain and maintain the levels of growth for our team. It is an awakening to be very alive and alert on this journey.

My Soul encourages:
Good, that is news to rejoice. With awareness comes the amazing empowerment of The ALL Source. I am predicting great strides forward for our team.

T) What is pulling Your Carriage?

The Angels of The Light continue:
A visual to pull this life adventure all together—this picture visual is uniquely yours—allow it to fit you perfectly.

Begin with the visual of a five-part harmony—your team of Soul—Mind—Ego—Body plus your Guardian Angels—together at the starting gate of your chosen journey of adventure there on earth.

Describe your pathway for your team—is it a maze—a labyrinth—a garden path—a hillside climb—a winding path of stones—a

Insight from the Heavens

walk along the beach—you select or invent your own pathway.

Are you stepping hand-in-hand with your team—are you sightseeing—are you in a parade—are you moving slowly—or racing to the finish line—does the pathway light up with each step you take—do you note your intended direction—or do you just wing it on this adventure?

Describe your team's actions—are you waving—smiling at others along the way—entertaining yourselves and others—oblivious of others—are you riding or walking—passing out gifts—throwing money or showering gold coins in your wake?

Has your team noted the signposts—or taken Side Ventures—Swing Exchange Ventures—Full Action Ventures—accessed the Withdrawal Choice—a Secondary/Shadow Path—chosen to Lift to Clarity—noted your Levels of Intention—engaged the Trust within Yourself—and/or retained focus on your Soul's Growth?

Your carriage awaits—what is pushing—pulling or engaging your team's forward movement? A team of horses—the harnessed strength of a wild animal—a wild stagecoach ride—a covered wagon—an elegant carriage—a fancy sports car—a stretch limousine—and are you driving or a passenger?

What colours surround your team? Dressed in your finest—a casual or uniform outfit—beachwear—formalwear—plush coloured velvet upholstery within your carriage—coloured streamers decorate your automobile—and what colour(s) is your team's selection of attire?

The end is in sight—the finish line—is it an altar—a garden—the pearly gates? What is your team doing? Giving high fives—holding huge beaming smiles—engaging in a four-part harmonizing of Hallelujahs or Amazing Grace songs—patting each other on the back—reviewing your accomplishments on your journey—releasing sighs of relief—or barely containing joyful anticipation to be showered within the heavenly ALL love—of the welcome celebration of a choirs of Angels and the Heavenly Family waiting to embrace your team in huge group hugs?

My Mind expresses:
Angels, this is a wonderful personal visualization that I am sure to enjoy experiencing in meditation. It fits your quote given to me many years ago and I share it here.

- ❖ **The Reflection of Today—is the Seeking of Tomorrow—The Angels of The Light.**

My Mind offers:
We can create and invent or recall the description of the path we take when the team is in place to engage the vision of the path.

- ❖ **Recap the Past—Re-forecast the Future—and Live in the Now—The Angels of The Light.**

My Mind expresses gratitude:
Thank you—these words seem to be not enough to

show appreciation for the assistance you offer on our soul journey. Angels, an attempt to express a never-ending appreciation for your guidance from The ALL Source may only offer this limited heart felt expression from my team however, we now add—*Love returned to you!*

The Angels of The Light accept:
You're welcome—it is our pleasure to guide you within The ALL love—we enjoy this task immensely—to add here—the review of the past is of insight when the focus is placed on intent—what did you intend to do—did you follow through—how did it effect you and others—in either case of follow through or not—what caused the lack of follow through—this is awareness to apply to the future intent for the empowerment of your journey there—it is to take the gift of choice and follow through on intent to the embrace of self in the connection of The ALL awareness—and remain alert to the flow of wonder—miracles—synchronicities—and abundance of life—know you are truly blessed and held in the total—eternal—and unconditional love of The ALL Source—your Guiding Angels of The Light.

U) Journey of Engagement of ALL Love:

As we begin here—it is of a journey to the engagement of ALL love we address—we are of the light—energy—and colour of ALL love vibrations—and it is to this engagement we do assist your awareness—it is to this awareness that it is a seeking to re-engage with intention on your path—and this enables the abundance of Soul growth.

It is in the encasing of your truth—your lifting of knowings—and the clarity of this knowledge—that we do assist in many ways—of which we have mentioned prior.

We also reach out to you during your carriage ride home—it is in these moments of intense clarity—that you are enveloped or surrounded within The ALL love—it is during these final days on earth—that your soul jumps into the lead—to lift the mind into this thought of ALL assistance—and into the acceptance of The ALL love.

As it is of resistance to some souls—who have followed paths of detours—and swing adventures—or of another's path focus—it can also be souls who have accepted the truths imposed upon their mind—without question—and quieted their own truth bells—it is these souls we carry toward the ALL Light—as an attempt to offer clarity during this final approach.

It is of an intense and a full-on illumination we offer—to display a quick study if you will—to the acceptance of their own chosen journey of rediscovery to The ALL love.

The gift of free will does remain with each team—and therefore the resistance to a new belief system—can be accepted or rejected during this final approach to The ALL love eternity—it is of no celebrating party that awaits those souls—as it has been their intense desire to maintain a system of belief that does not include The ALL love—their journey is ended with a guided tour into a review station—and an opportunity to gain illumination on their next journey of soul growth—as they again prepare the details of their next itinerary of soul growth—and incarnation to the guiding steps of editing and changes in The ALL love wisdom—another journey of rediscovery awaits them within an incarnation journey—with the support of another team of Mind—Ego—and Angels.

It is of many choices and selection again prepared to offer direction—assistance—and to highlight a renewed clarity—to the chosen Overview Mission of Intent along with their Purpose and Approach in place—to assist others as well as Preserve Self on this new itinerary.

We say here further—these souls are wiser with each incarnation—and thereby create an intricate and detailed itinerary—to enable an efficient rediscovery of The ALL love—this renewed intention is assisted and guided during the debriefing process here in heaven—and assistance to their planning is in abundance as the heavens offer ALL wisdom of The ALL insight—to assist their plan—and this is the approach offered to the planning of all itineraries for soul growth.

As it is to the Souls who resist The ALL love acceptance that we do speak of here—it is also of the souls who choose to remain in the comfort of a negative stronghold—as in crime and harm to others—as they relish the power of this control to strip other souls of their free will and choice gifts—for these souls the return to the heavens is a quick and swiftly directed—temporary stop to a holding space—where they are offered the opportunity to clarity of The ALL love—with the assistance to leap into the positive and illuminated vision of an ALL love unconditional love.

It is during this holding detention—that the magnitude of their choices on earth are reviewed—in a rewind for these souls—and the positive approach of their actions displayed to offer a clarity of the choices they made during the past incarnation.

Should these souls retain their heavy negative thought pattern of free choice—they then prepare a movement into another chamber space of darkness—and this then leads to a multiple movement into connecting chambers—that gradually become lighter and lighter with an attempt to lift their choices into lightness—and a return to The ALL love sustenance.

On rare occasions a soul does not respond to this ALL Light—and is guided to a placement of pre-planning—a return to soul growth with heightened attention given to the team and players to assist on the path—players selected for the soul growth earth journey fitting into the old soul category of wisdom to assist a renewed journey.

The unconditional ALL love does engage everlasting love to every soul—and does also assist with a never-ending intention to lift each soul into illumination of The ALL Source.

Yes—a win-win approach with the utmost patience is The ALL love intention.

It is of a huge celebration we do remind you here—that is displayed to the souls who have gained illumination on their paths—and lifted their ALL love connection on the earth adventure—as it is a path of guided assistance to all souls—it is also a welcome of a return home beyond your imagination—as you are wrapped within and embraced by The ALL love—it is a celebration of your Heavenly Family that you are blessed and lifted into the joy and lightness of your ALL energies.

My Mind visualizes:
Something to really look forward to! The celebration of our Soul's growth journey with the gain of illumination to the path and the connection to The ALL love is going to be fantastic!

The Angels of The Light confirm:
Yes—it is certainly something to look forward to—at the completion of your soul itinerary tasks of focused soul growth on earth—with the return home.

V) Our Soul Family on Earth:

As it is now clearer to you the aspects of your soul's return to the Heavenly family—it is also our desire to assist your embrace of your Earthly soul family—that are in place to assist your achievement to soul growth there.

We do say here—to offer you further clarity—the selection of your family—and the friends on your path—that appear to be an external support family—has been carefully selected by you—the soul for your team adventure—you have also selected your Form—for the convenience to your intention—and your Mind is prepped to receive the information of this learning adventure you have chosen—as well as the selection of your Ego is predesigned.

Yes—it is all predesigned in intricate detail—as mentioned prior—when the selection of your Form or Body is taken into observation during your itinerary layout—it is to all the probable and possible scenarios that you play out prior to the final selection—with this valuable information laid out before you—and the guidance offered of insight of The ALL love—you determine and select the Body or Form for your earthly adventure—this then begins an ever-important focus to the self-preservation intention to this Body of choice—and one not taken lightly—therefore—this insight here does offer to you the acceptance and renewed desire to protect and preserve this Body—as an important aspect to the containing of your Soul—for the duration of this journey.

This preservation of the Body or Form chosen is to be an ongoing challenge—as you move forward—as it does challenge the Mind to nurture and protect its automatic functions—and needs to carry the team of Soul—Mind—Ego to completion.

The choices are of huge importance in the preplanning—as well as the execution of the plan—during incarnation—the Mind does reside within the head of the Form—and it is given the basics of operations to engage further Soul growth—in example—similar to the hard drive programming of a computer—yes—and you then engage the adventure of Soul growth there on earth—the Mind is your vision board on your journey there—you could compare this to your monitor screen of the computer—for this example—yes—the Mind does engage this visual display during your day and an inner display during your dreams—it is a task of automatic response—and the awareness of this does then engage the memory and recall availability—access you retain to assist clarity on your path chosen.

As it is part of the Team that is designed to assist your journey—and take you to the final days here on earth—it is of importance to also protect and nurture in the choice of thoughts retained—to assist forward movement of Soul growth in the positive intention—the Mind is placed to absorb and listen to the wisdom of the Soul—and to engage the support of the Ego—yes—your Ego is also selected for the qualities of self-motivation and self-preservation to the team of Soul—Mind—and Ego—plus the Body—in the aspect of appearance—the Ego resides just below the Mind—and is twined with the Mind in the focus of preservation and motivation intention of success on your chosen path of soul growth—the Ego however—does desire to have its voice heard—and this is evident at times throughout your desires for achievement of earthly display to material gains—and body preservation at heightened levels of attainment—these times of Ego control are key times to clue into the need for balanced team talk—as the Ego has stepped outside the description of its positive motivation and preservation focus.

The Ego is described as the motivator and preserver of the team approach—to your adventure there—it is a powerful tool of ALL energy—that is placed within your Body—to assist a gift of motivating and self-preservation from The ALL love—it is wise to check in with your Ego—and thereby ensures your team voice remains in balance during your journey there.

Your Ego is a gift of energy from The ALL Source—as is your Body or Form—your Mind is a pre-programmed gift of directional approach of positive—unconditional love energy of The ALL Source—and your Soul—as mentioned prior—is a gifted adventure companion of ALL Source energies of intention to engage illuminated growth to acceptance of ALL love.

Your Soul is of The ALL energies—and remains eternally—totally and unconditionally within and of The ALL love.

The pre-design of your itinerary for your earthly journey—does enable your Soul to choose the team of assistance—with the Body—the Mind—and the Ego—and also the intricate detailing of its itinerary of growth—to foresee any possible or probable event and action or reaction—it is to this attention to detail we do offer further insight with the selection of your Earth Family of Souls—also preset and selected to play out their parts within your earth adventure there.

It is to the intention to engage growth—in the aspect of love in ALL Source magnificence and magnitude—that the intention for your journey is set out—your family—your friends—your pre-arranging of helpful people souls—are also chosen prior to birth—as noted before—these souls also retain their free will and may choose to not follow through with this pre-accepted part they agreed to play out in connection to your path—as this can then create Side Ventures—Swing Exchange Ventures—and Withdrawals—as noted prior here—however—these other souls on your path may have only agreed to shift you into another direction—and play their agreed parts perfectly—to offer you new insight or prevent you from taking a detour or move into a construction hurdle to overcome—therefore—they are of predesigned assistance—these people are helpers and assist you by offering insight example—and a lesson or reason for their presence on your path—this is worthy of an introspective review—to your gain of growth.

There are Souls who are predesigned to

assist your soul growth for only a short time—or a season you say there—and these Souls do also play out exactly the pre-written part accepted to assist your soul growth—these Souls leave behind an impact of important message—that can be positive or negative—for your observation and reflection.

As we move now into the pre-design aspect of your soul growth itinerary—where the Souls accept a position of moving along your journey with you until completion—these Souls can engage your path at many different points or intersections—as do the other Souls mentioned—however—these Souls connect with you on a deep level of knowing—they appear to really know and accept you in a soul growth connection—these Souls remain to assist your growth—or to support and motivate your movement forward to completion—you do acknowledge their assistance with a returned recognition of their Soul needs—and do mutually assist their path of soul growth as well—this does lift to you the addition of further assistance to your journey of growth on earth—that has been pre-selected and agreed upon.

W) Intersection of Distraction:

Now we speak of the Intersection of Distraction to your path there—these events that are of unplanned or unexpected detours—when a rouge of Souls detour from their path's pre-arranged itinerary—and engage in an energy of negative movement to initiate a tidal wave of sweeping other Souls off their paths of intention—this can be an entanglement of free will on the part of some Souls—and a surprisingly strong pull to other Souls.

We do offer this example here—of an unexpected opportunity presented with the dangling of something too good to be true—in a material sense—or a momentum of persuasive reason—that is guarded—and resistant to offering any explanation that lifts to your truth inner bell of knowing and your position of balance with your Mind and Ego—can determine the involvement to this Intersection of Distraction you do experience. *(A time when alertness to your intuition can prevent a group or person who manipulates and controls the free-will of others, becoming a part of our lives. No questions are permitted to enable access to one's free-will in these cases. Then it really is too good to be true.)*

Yes—it is to the full view of opportunity that is recommended—with a turning up of your Soul voice volume—as your inner bell of truth rings clearly for you.

It is in clarity of the assistance of ALL love gifted to you on your journey there—that does engage your action to remain or return to a positive and balanced soul growth—in an ease of movement—with synchronicity of events assisting the illumination of your best choices.

We do move now from this Intersection of Distraction—to an Intersection of Attraction.

X) Intersection of Attraction:

This is of a descriptive to note to self there—as this intersection displays a positive forward movement—it is displayed with an engagement of ease for you—it is ease of movement to the use of your gifts of talents and traits—and also openly displays a fit to your intention of soul growth—in the signs of team balance—to gains of insight.

This example we offer here—an opportunity is given to express your inner Soul voice—in a positive display like a stage presentation of your skills to assist others—and expand the assistance to a world stage—or to a unique and interested smaller audience of like minds—as it is a clear and precise offer to expand your vision of soul growth—your inner knowing of truth rings loud—and triggers your attention to this offer of growth for your Soul.

This can be monetary and can lead to a new level of insight—yes—and it can be only of further exposure to your intention soul growth message—that engages the minds of other Souls—in a guidance to the ALL love awareness—or it can be both monetary growth—to enable your comfort ability to reach out further—or to engage your Overview Mission of assistance—to offering Example—to Share insight—to Inspire others to reach for ALL Love—to Teach the path of best—or to Heal others—enabling them to move into a positive and empowered renewal of Soul growth.

It is a clarity of the ALL love you do intend

Insight from the Heavens

to focus attentions to re-engaging—it is of this thought that will assist your choices of best—listen to your wise Soul—your truth bell—and the balanced voice of positive self-preservation from the twin voices of Mind and Ego—in unison—as you are guided by The ALL love and vibrations of Angels on your path—we are all in place for your access—always available on your path of predesigned growth to return to The ALL love awareness and acceptance.

It is with this glimpse of the assistance available to you there—that you are held and assisted in The ALL love blessings—and journey forward in Lightness and Joy.

Y) An Expression of Passion:

It is of a journey that the tasks align to your focus and Overview Mission—it is to this focus and passion of task that we speak of here—a passion is a drive that captures your interest—it does engage your Mind and Ego to work together—and completes the team effort with gain of growth for the Soul.

A passion is described as a desire or intent to accomplish a task that holds your interest—and motivates you into action—it is of this desire to place self into an Example of ability to display—or a desire to research and Share—or to engage in the inspiration of task or intention—or give attention to detail in Teaching knowledge—or an attempt to Heal self or others with application of proven techniques of preventative medicines or non-medical approaches.

These areas of your Overview Missions will drive your passion and these tasks of interest will lead you to the jobs or projects that capture your Mind and Ego—to move forward with the gain of further soul growth.

We give examples here—as you gain in desire to express self—you will give Examples of this expression in the application of self in project completion of a creative nature—in home or in assisting others—the desire to Share does lift to you a need to engage others with the information you have contained within your Mind and this drives you to offer of self in the world stage or on the home front—does offer satisfaction of this passion—as a passion to Teach others to growth within does display a focus to organization of your skills—so does the passion to enable the Healing of souls—and offer clarity of the needs of the Body that drives this passion.

As it is of a view from above this observation does lift to you—the focused passion you have chosen to engage on your path there—it is of this Overview clarity you will engage an ability to achieve great strides forward on your adventure there.

We do now move to the Expression of Passion in an engagement to the ALL love—we begin to give you to the importance of this Overview Mission as it does lift your clarity to the ALL love.

The view of your journey to this point

is a guide to you—it is of this view you are to determine your passion and it is of this view you do reflect on the approach taken in an unaware movement to engaging your Overview Mission—this approach enables you to see clearly your past performance that will propel your present action and future attempts to soul growth.

The Soul is engaged with the Mind and Ego—as it is a joint venture you are experiencing—this venture is filled with opportunities to gain clarity and direct the forward movement of your Soul.

We are to open here to you a path of acceleration—when the clarity of your Overview Mission is gained—it is awareness of a direction of insight—and an observation of a release to fill all the five areas of choice with a relief and release of weight that has been taken on by some souls driven to achieve—it is with this release of a need to attempt all missions that your Soul does lift to your ear—a clarity of path to engage your self-preservation and self-motivation—to excel in the focus of one Overview Mission—this clarity to path does then lift to you a clarity to the vision of ALL love—this is an illumination of the attention to success and inspiration to attain an exemplary intention—to the gain of awareness of soul growth—in the clarity of the use of talents and traits—in use—to enable achievement of your focus within the ALL love energies of insight. *(Choose to remember the ONE Overview Mission that was chosen prior to birth, to empower your team. It may appear that several will fit you, however, the selection of only one is the suggestion here.)*

As it is of clarity you seek—it is of clarity we offer here—allow your Overview Mission to capture your motivational drive—to lift yourself to see clearly the intent you choose to express on this life adventure to soul growth.

It is of this action you move into the simplicity of the adventure—and clarity of focus enabling you to gain The ALL love awareness in large strides forward.

This will then lift to you the joy and lightness of your journey there—with a singular focus to all tasks.

Z) An Area of Humour:

Now we move to the Area of Humour—it is to the joy and lightness that enables a building of rhythm—and engages your awareness of abundance of synchronicities placed throughout your journey there.

The lightness of positive humour is engaging to your team—it is an exercise to lift and to release—this is noted in the brief explosions of laughter—or belly laughs you say there—it is the release of the Body to stored up doubts and worries that block the path and vision to forward movement—it is the trigger of the laughter release valve—we do encourage to maintain a balanced approach to your path—as it does lift the listening ability gifts of your team—it is in the humour of the moment—or

Insight from the Heavens

the engagement to take self less seriously—that does embrace the blessings of ALL love to your Team.

The humour of the moment is the lightness of step—the smile lifted to your face—the release of worry to your Mind—and the expression of your Ego to assist in harmony—as your Team moves forward into lightness.

This expression of laughter releases desires to engage in the building up of explosive verbal or physical frustration—it is when the placement of self within a spring wound too tightly—that the need for release is necessary in a positive expression of laughter—as well as for example—when motivation is desired to enable an action to express self fully—it is wise to engage in positive humour.

- ❖ Laughter is the Movement of Unconditional Love through the Body. This is very Healing—The Angels of The Light.

Here is a bit of humour with The ALL/and the Angels!

My Mind recalls:
This heavenly humour was presented to me late one evening as I was finishing preparation for an upcoming event. I re-read the page of information on the computer screen while it was printing off. *Oh that is odd, I noted.* Throughout the entire typed information displayed on the monitor, wherever the small word *up* was typed, a number 7 was boldly standing in front of it. Quickly retrieving the copy from the printer I burst out laughing, as there was

not a **7-UP** to be found on the printed copy. A great release of divine humour, just when I needed it!

Section 6: The Expression of Emotions:

We do move now into the Expression of Emotions—the emotions of application on your journey there are abundant—it is of a need to engage your motivation—and also your self-preservation that the use of emotions captures there.

On the path of insight—your engaging of emotions are a necessary gain and do propel forward as well as detour movement.

It is to this we speak of further here—the emotions are placed in groups of four and the first set of emotions take in your expression of self with the Emotions of Love—Praise—Joy and Insight—as positive self -preservation emotions.

The second set of Emotions is the opposite of the aforementioned—with a Sadness—an Anger—and an Emotion of Mistrust—in a negative expression.

The third group of Emotions include a Motivating expression—with Aggression to control—to Harbour Threats—and to Gain Superiority.

As is the fourth set of Emotions—the opposite to the above in Motivating expression to the positive approach of Assertive Movement— with others' needs included—the Emotion to Include the Interest of others—in a group effort engagement—and to Retain Balanced

position of Equality—in the awareness of ALL One on this journey.

These Emotions do open further to you the focus of needed motivation and self-preservation in a positive forward journey—experienced in joy and lightness.

As we express here prior—it is enlightenment to your gifted choices and options—that allows your expressions in the grace of ALL love—and it is this insight that your journey there was built on—in preparation of your itinerary.

We do encourage your awareness to the Emotions you choose to express or access as you journey there—it is of the gifted free will you do access—and retain the option of choice to excel with your selections—or stall yourself with a negative choice—your clarity to path does assist in the choices of best—as you engage and absorb this insight to The ALL Source—and design of your chosen path.

a. Take Your Emotional Pulse:

It is of a glimpse you can gain in checking your Emotional Pulse—this is a use of your observations and directing them to a lifting of self above yourself—to observe and note the emotion you are presently choosing to express—and also the degree you are expressing this emotion—simply put—you become aware instantly of the presentation you have selected to play out your emotions—and this could be in a withdrawal/aloof presentation—a overly zealous exaggeration—a verbal expression of insults/impact words/actions—a position/ body stance of intimidation—or the move into a lengthy pity party for one—to describe a few of the negative choices that put up blocks to your forward movement.

When recognition is observed—your emotional pulse is also displayed in the speed up of adrenalin that could be harmful to the body—also the view of consequence or repercussion is instantly offered in this private vision—we hold the mirror for you at these times with encouragement to ask yourself—is there a better response or venting release that I could choose here—is this a repetitive stumbling block—what has caused this inner turmoil—am I fearful of being blocked or lost in a re-run of interaction?

In the wisdom of the universal ALL love— there is always a purpose—choose to move into the lift and acceptance of heavenly illuminated assistance to make better choices for your team and remove the repetitious stumbling blocks as you take the observer seat in taking your emotional pulse.

As the trust is placed in the thoughts of the Mind with ability to access changes to positive self-empowerment—the touch within of this emotional pulse enables the pull to the surface for examination—which guides to the reason of this display of emotions—the desire of the Soul is to express and reflect itself—ending the struggle—the message presented is to a positive and empowered team preservation that reflects an inner and

outer view. *(A trust in one's ability to lift for recognition, the underlying motivation for each overly emotion reaction displayed.)*

Angels alert us to take our Emotional Pulse!

My Mind requests:
This would be good to note if I am acting or reacting from a love base or a fear base. Can you jump in on this awareness, Soul, and lift your voice for my observation? Taking this emotional pulse in observation of current expression of choice is a practise I want to take place in my daily life.

My Soul offers:
You got it, I would love to engage the Mind of this team adventure to the emotions experiencing in

an observation any time you are open to ask for my input.

The Angels of The Light explain:

This action of checking your Emotional Pulse does offer a gauge or tool of insight to enable you to adjust the level of your emotional experience—or to choose to change the emotion altogether—and avoiding a following consequence that can lead to harm to your Body—or a verbal statement that sets up reaction from others in return.

As you check your Emotional Pulse—you can physically note your blood pressure—as it becomes elevated when an emotion of negativity begins to grow—or the celebration of a wonderful surprise event takes place in your life—it is essential to monitor your emotions to gauge your balance of Mind—Ego and Body for the optimal maintenance to the team harmony.

Emotions are expressed in a full range— reaching a high level of volume—or can access the lower level of volume—it is suggested that mid-range is a healthy level mentally and physically with the exception of singing praise or hallelujahs—as you gain awareness of your ability to regulate your emotions—you can lift to self the emotions you desire to retain in your tool chest of assistance to you on your path there.

b. Lifting Self into Observation of The ALL Unconditional Love:

It is of a gentle approach to the next step

Insight from the Heavens

here we do offer to you—illumination of the task of lifting self into observation of ALL love—and a visit to The ALL Source space of unconditional love—you are held within and of this space always—however you are unaware of this level of engagement to The ALL love until you lift the veil of forgetfulness—to take a glimpse for yourself.

As it is offered to you at all times to engage this view—it is your own desire that it will motivate the taking of the next step—we do wrap you within the safety of The ALL Source—as you move into this lightness of love and joy.

To prepare yourself for this short journey—it is wise to engage the openness of thoughts and just begin to allow yourself to embrace peace and fulfillment—it is with these emotions in place—you can relax into a review of your desires to gain clarity—and then begin to visualize—or allow yourself to dream vision—or astral travel—these short adventures do occupy an open and empty mind of no prior conception of your glimpse of the heavens—as it is to a new look here—you are offered to refresh your memory.

The assistance of guided meditations of gratitude and intent can assist you there—however it can be a simplistic desire to see clearly your life purpose and overview mission—or to engage both in clarity—as you choose the approach note that as you call in The ALL love—you will be engaged and wrapped in Angel hugs as it is of this protection to your team that is assisted—then just let go of your thoughts and wait with a pen/pencil and pad to write upon placed within your grasp—it is that easy and can be a very quick visit—or a lingering tour of the heavens—as you engage an Angel sightseeing group of visitors—we are there with you always—and it is to this thought you maintain your safety net—to gently place you back on earth.

Now as it is a view of heavens you seek—it is the taking of self onto the craft of choice—as in flight and speed required and chosen—you can choose a glimpse of this heavenly place—or you can choose to engage the tour—it is always your choice—and your choice to end this visual trip—as your Soul becomes your guide and the Ego and Mind do tag along—your body remains here on earth as your anchor to return to the adventure of Soul growth here with renewed vigour and insight.

This heavenly visit is a choice you retain always—and a choice you can access at any time during the soul growth experience.

Now we express the action of falling into an abyss—this is the fear of not completing the journey to glimpse The ALL Source heavenly space—it is a worry of safety and guidance you are choosing to embrace here—this visual concept of television and movies of the falling action—and loss of control that aligns with fear—and it is a false concept that has been ingrained with memory recall of your birthing experience—as we explain here—the only access of falling is the movement of the soul into the body for the duration of your soul growth journey—all other movement is elevated—a lifting upward into the spaces of welcome centers if you will—to the level of growth of soul accommodation.

We do also say here—the level of heaven is always within your grasp—and is the next level to attain when leaving your earth journey—it is an access of a short trip home and is reached in a direct route to the ALL love—as the soul is lifted with the rewind of your golden/silver cord of attachment to the ALL Source—by example here—just as your intentions and thoughts are of your connection and ownership there—the ALL Source is the connection and retains ownership of soul energy—you are given this lift up at your choosing—and or at divine timing—as in your best interest.

The fear of this process of a return to the heavens—or of a visit to the heavens—does conjure up the emotion of fear for many minds there—and this is a result of absorbing a presentation of memory recall—replayed within the mind—as an imbalance to the ease of movement aspect is not highlighted to replace the memory selection—it is the ease of movement that is the suggested update to install in your memory—the carrying of an emotion of fear does not engage an open mind—and prevents your movement of level growth for the soul.

Clear out your old concepts—as they no longer work for you—as you reach the level of joy and lightness—and allow your Mind to be open and free to absorb only your truth—as it listens for the individual truth bell ring or sound.

Section 7: Answers from The Angels— Our Mission Companions:

Eight Levels of Angels with Selected Categories:

There are eight levels of Angels—five that the work is with the souls who incarnate—and three that observe as in the presence of The ALL—the Angels of The Light that you work with are in the category level of Joy—there is also Peace—then Love—Trust and the Selection of Insight categories—as each soul's journey is unique—it is to each predesigned itinerary that the selection of Angels do match the soul's choice of focus—as to the levels—we say that Insight are of the highest—then the Peace and Joy—and Love and Trust—we are of the five groups that work with souls who incarnate and on the colour of our wings—we are of multi-illuminating colours—a reflection of the rainbow—as to exact colour—it is of course a discretion on our part as to a presentation of any one colour according to our work with you—our wings will reflect the observation of the individual soul's main purpose there—we can show our wings or not—it is our choice—we are now showing you blue with assistance to engaging your mission—many opportunities of Joy await.

It is clarity you seek to have—and to give to assist others—it is of this we do engage through you with the portraits and into messages—in most cases it is true that we Angels have not incarnated—we are of a full joy and thereby other emotions do not enter—however we do have empathy of the emotions in ranges you do suffer—we are very much approachable and are of the vibrations of The ALL—it is in this we do lead in the warmth of welcome to all energy souls—we are your Mission Companions.

Your Spirit Guide does open to you the best path of every day—and does assist in your comprehension and direction of thought—your Angels are of assistance to you in preparing the path of best—and we do surround you in The ALL love—you are aware of us on an external level—and also there in your subconscious level—on the birth level you retain this awareness—prior to accepting the veil of forgetfulness.

The Soul is covered in a light of protection prior to rebirth—as encased within The ALL hand of protection—it is in this colour of yellow light the soul is held during your reincarnation—your aura of coloured energy surrounds your body—and the first level is the white light of ALL Source—a combination of all colours—the display of additional colours reflect the emotions you experience and will change as you engage additional or different emotions—research into these colours will assist your insight and the observation of our Angel energy that dances within these colours—as we stay ever so near your soul growth.

Angel light and guidance to empowerment and joy of expression of self on the path chosen—will be expressed within the colours of each portrait as we will be setting a mark for you to point out and highlight—this is a signature mark of the Artist and Spirit Guide of these portraits—we are The Angels of The Light and do facilitate this mark—your Spirit is a guide to you and your Soul is there on a journey of growth.

We are the glow of light—the energy of flight—and the embrace of colour—we can take on any form of earthly communication to alert and reach out to guide you—we are assigned the task of assistance and guidance in all areas of your life—with direction to your best interest—always—we shower upon you the unconditional—eternal—and total Love of The ALL Source with the focus to lift your gifted awareness—you are blessed with gifts and talents and abundant choices to assist your journey to a successful completion—you can set up a personal Angel Alert recognition—to lift your awareness in the selection of one of your six senses.

Lift and explore this path with wonder and selections of best in ALL love—discover your somewhat hidden clues of insight—you are of The ALL as we do celebrate and engage—

your Angels of The Light—you have chosen to reach the level of Joy on your mission focus—remember—Joy is your calling card, Gloria—as you absolutely do have friends in high places.

My Mind is overflowing:
This continuous insight from The Angels of The Light offers clarity to inspire. And yet there is so much more to hear. No wonder my Mind could not retain all this information during my visit to heaven. It is a huge download of insight. Must save on my Mind's external hard drive, for security I think.

Section 8: Selection of Passion: (Joy—Peace—Trust):

The Angels of The Light continue:
We speak here about a Selection of Passion—as the Mission Overview is chosen to serve as an umbrella type of observation tool—in application to your intentions there—the choice of passion is related to the focus to maintaining a positive emotion choice and a protective emotion for forward movement.

As mentioned prior here—we Angels align with a positive emotion and this alignment is focused with the passion of the soul we assist during their earth adventure—in your case, Gloria—you chose the passion of Joy and this is what we align with to assist your focus to maintain this emotion.

Many other Souls choose the other Positive emotions of Peace or Trust—it is then a focus for their path to align with this emotion—we will assist every soul with the focus to their selected passion. A Passion choice is suggested when a soul's itinerary appears overloaded during the planning stage—and as it continues through the review process—suggestions are made by the review team in their heavenly wisdom—for adjustment and changes—to garner an attainable success application probability—for the adventure about to jump into.

We do add here—it is of a selection that lifts the load and therefore one of the positive emotions—it is to this your journey lifts to a successful attainable outcome—as to the passion you take on—it is of a full load of itinerary items that does engage this passion—and it will also align with your chosen Mission.

This Passion is the motor so to say—that will assist a forward movement—as it drives you to fulfill this passion during your selected journey and entries on your itinerary to engage this passion in all your choices there—and therefore—it is a clue to you to recognize when selecting choices on your path—to check that these choices align with your Passion.

My Mind remembers:
When attending our Church's Sunday school during my youth, I was always excited when our class occasionally attended a portion of the adult service. We would march single file from the social room to then occupy the reserved up front pews in the church congregation hall. I am sure the hymns were chosen with these little ones in mind and we eagerly participated. I am now recalling one joyful

song. This song would begin with the lyrics *I've got Joy, Joy, Joy down in my heart* - then some adult would yell out *Where?* - We'd all respond - *Down in my heart!* This chorus was repeated several times and the spontaneity of the congregation would lift giggles from us children and encourage the search for the person who yelled this playful question—*Where? A fun memory of the emotion of joy I now understand to be the motor that propels my team's passion and maintains a space of residence down in my heart!* The image of an attainable stretch to seek joy in all future choices for our team is remarkable to me.

Section 9: Time as Compared to No-Time:

As it is clear to us here—it is time to move into the description of no-time. Yes—we play here with these words and thoughts—your concept of time on earth does not exist here in heaven—it is a controlled environment you do engage in there—and this is a concept that assists your visualizing of movement there—as you appear to progress with a set itinerary—and this is all part of the playing out of the adventure you have chosen to experience.

It is a unique concept given to earth with all the levels of challenge and focuses to maintain—there is a need filled there with the time frame sections and the breaking down to minutes and seconds—then extending to decades and centuries—and then eons of time—the need filled is a tool offered—to assist you to gauge your movement there—to

use the review technique individually—and thereby take note of your achievements and success.

Time does not exist here in the heavens—it does not require a need to engage the control of movement—or the noting of growth—time appears to stand still during your visits here—and you could say it does—however it is non-existent.

In this heavenly space—there is no past or future experienced—only the space of now—this space contains the fulfillment and gains of all incarnation of each Soul's journey—and allows the absorption of additional growth without the marker of time applied.

We add further here—a journey in time is an incarnation on Earth School—there are unique attributes to other school adventures—however time remains unique to the Earth School—as the chosen itinerary of events and the challenges of missions and passions applied and experienced there—you have chosen this unique adventure on earth to fine-tune your Soul growth—and expand your ALL awareness.

It is a celebration we do express to you—as your earth adventure is completed—however passing out of caps and gowns will not be part of the celebration—the full-on celebration of heavenly family partying will be your experience—to the anticipation of your soul and level of growth attained—we will bring out the rainbows for you to touch—just to give you a glimpse of the party favours here.

My Mind responds:
I would love to touch the rainbows. And they are only a glimpse of the party favours in heaven. Such a wonderful place makes me wonder, with the piling on of challenges here to focus on and experience in a desire to gain soul growth, why would we choose to put ourselves through this Earth School with all the selections to experience and surmount? Why not just stay and grow my soul in Heaven? It seems like a fun place to be.

Section 10: Incarnation—A Bigger Picture:

The Angels of The Light explain:
As we begin here—it is of a need now to describe the big picture further—your desire to incarnate on earth is a choice you made after much deliberation—and also the engaging of council team in heaven—that offers support and suggestions of best—to assist your decision—it is a decision not taken lightly and it is a decision made to access an opportunity for quick growth for your Soul.

You are of a young soul when you decide to incarnate and with each incarnation—you achieve further understanding to the big picture of soul growth and the ALL awareness—it is to the combination of youth and adventure that you select the incarnation approach—and as you gain the knowledge of repetitive incarnations—your wisdom gain is settled into a wise soul category—at that time the need for speed and adventure is not priority to you—and the slower gathering of growth in the heavens is agreeable to you.

You know the saying—*absence makes the heart grow fonder*—this is a reflection of choice to leave the knowledge of The ALL to place yourself blindly into another space to participate in the process of recall—and lifting the blinders you then return with the gained awareness to The ALL Source and into the space of ALL Love.

There are many choices available here in heaven for soul growth—as well as on earth—it is the desire to gain The ALL vision from a perceived distance that does facilitate your Earth School.

The application to soul growth here in heaven is more of fine-tuning—and offering you detailed understanding of the basic inquiries of ALL love that is the curriculum for the Earth School.

We do say here further—you do require the basics to excel to a level of excellence—and this Earth School does offer this basic—plus the adventure of forgetfulness in an itinerary-directed play of events to lead you back into awareness—this is laid out by you—and given review and guidance from the heavenly souls of wisdom here—to adjust and assist its success as previously mentioned—then off you go to experience this chosen adventure—with the assistance in place from The ALL love.

Remember—you are never left alone there—you are surrounded with heavenly assistance

Insight from the Heavens

to reach out to and accept the love of The ALL Source—your choice to reincarnate is individual—and is selected to fit your desires to improve your Soul wisdom—there are many areas there on earth to gain wisdom in study and application of experience and you do access these as well at your choosing.

Variety is the spice of life—it is said and can be compared to the choices in abundance available to you here and there—it is an earth incarnation that does offer you a memory of home—and this is comforting during your times of forgetfulness there—these comforts are oblivious to you at times—and also very clearly déjà vu to you at times of clarity.

Your trip away from home—does also engage your delight to return to this ALL love space of heaven—you do also delight in the taking on this earth adventure—and then relish the return home—and the celebration you walk into—so to speak.

We offer you this visual—as your Soul leaves the Body or form—it is grateful for the shelter and the two friends of the Mind and Ego as to their role played in this adventure—should the adventure be ended on the positive note—the good-byes are heartfelt—if not on a positive note—regrets will linger within the Soul—as to the unsuccessful aspects that may have been—in the selection of better choices and also expression or application.

Your incarnation choices remain with you—in all aspects—prior to and during your Earth School adventure—it is only your protection assistance and guidance that is gifted to you from The ALL Source.

This assistance is gifted with the free will choices—the talents and traits to assist your success—and guidance to your best choices—and are highlighted in many ways for your observation—plus The ALL protection of your souls intention and energies—as a part or piece of The ALL Source—you are never alone.

This does offer again a glimpse of your desire to reincarnate—expansion on this will be offered to you in the future there.

Section II: A Journey of Expression:

It is of a move now to offer you understanding to the expression of a Journey of Expression—it is evident now to you that an abundance of choices are gifted to your use there—it is important to express here—that the use of your gift of choice to engage forward movement for your Soul growth is encouraged within The ALL love—the expression of your soul is of the highest priority there—as it does facilitate growth—and when choices are made in the positive focus—huge gains result—these gains are felt and absorbed within your soul—they are contained to accelerate your positive forward insight.

As we do present here to you—the aspect of forward gains—we do however express the movement of backward as well—as choices again influence your movement—when they are accessed and applied in the negative—the

Soul—your Soul is placed in an open exposure to this negativity—and again it does present and lead to further regression in most cases—when the negative path is chosen—the negative choices breed negative response and consequence—as do the positive choices breed positive responses and consequences—as it is of importance here to point this out—it is also of assistance to you to recognize the category of your choices—at the time of selection.

Each choice comes with a possible gain to you in soul growth—and does move you forward to absorption of this gain—however if your choice offers or leads to a backward movement—the result of an unsuccessful and unfulfilling gain will result.

The choice is always given with highlight—to the best choice for forward movement on your path—however you also retain the choice to ignore—to block—or to not access this guiding information—and wing it on your own—so to add a visual here.

The choices of best are the highlighted observations given to your access of your six-sense knowing—it is the truth bell that rings—the sound of those little voices in your head—the feelings of safety or caution—the engaging of The ALL love and Angel hugs—these are the clues to a choice of best—as you open to the heavenly assistance—and open to your team with a positive balance—your soul voice will sing to you—the mind. The results being that you unlock the holds upon the soul

and allow it to engage the driver position on your journey—and this does lead to a simplistic flow of divine timing events unfolding for your observation daily—your choices become easier as you welcome input from your team of players—with a positive focus—you begin to soar there and the adventure becomes more fulfilling and exciting—you then move into your intended and predesigned soul growth itinerary—and become aware of the need for each entry with a passion of acceptance and insight gain.

You are offered guidance always—it is your choice to access and apply this heavenly wisdom.

Section 12: Gifted Talents, Traits, and Abilities:

We continue here ... it is to a comfort of a level of information we provide here—it is to this level of comfort it varies—the reader of this book we do wish to offer all degrees of insight—to enable all readers to gain understanding—and will continue of this approach in information offered of the Earth School there.

As we carry forward the thoughts of pre-designing one's life adventure there in itinerary format with event entries—and the pre-planning of all possible and probable free will accessible choices to each soul there—it is of a continuation of the overview we offer here.

A look within is a reflection of the look without—by this we speak of your designed

Insight from the Heavens

adventure along with your Traits—and your Abilities—and your gifted Talents.

The Talents are to assist your forward movement of soul growth—and are an extra push given to each soul—to assist in your self-motivation.

Your Traits are fine-tuned and some of this work is done prior to incarnation—and some of it during your exposure to family and your environment there.

Your Abilities are linked with both of the above Traits and Talents—your abilities are the expression and use of your Talents to the degree of choice focused on fine-tuning there—and the Traits are included in the Abilities with the engaging of learned application and lessons from the environment exposed to—as well as the observation of family.

The need for all three of these aspects of your personality—do lift to you when a full view is undertaken of your life there—this is done through the practice of meditation—or via a near-death experience—as you describe it—or a visitation to the heavens—as we describe it.

A successful lifting of this awareness to self—fulfills a necessary application of the choice to observe self—this self is your Team—of your Soul—and Mind—plus Ego—and Body does also offer a reflective quality to the tying together of this review—in that it does facilitate your comfort level—and your choice to access or terminate the review.

This is presented to your observation

by the comfort level of the Body during meditation—or a visit to the heavens—and also by the ability to continue Soul safety and protection—should the Body by example—be unable to withstand the meditation process of stillness—or the hyper-venting during some heavenly visits—the Body's balance will reflect this—this then is an observation to initiate the choice of a Team effort to focus attention of the health and vitality of the Body.

As for the observation platform of choice—this is made by each individual Soul—the degree of access to this insight varies—and relates directly to the degree of curiosity of the seeker—the insight gain of the Soul's chosen personality will open an observation of Traits and Talents to the choice of action or reaction—this then will assist the Soul's ability to express guidance and understanding to the Mind and Ego—therefore allowing a swing into either choice of action or reaction.

The Traits of the soul are the probability of action or reaction to any given event on the itinerary—and your soul does prepare the probability and possibility contingent plan for both—the awareness to the soul's traits response is an open window of opportunity to make a more productive choice—or stay within the safety of the status quo—or comfort zone of reaction.

Each encounter—triggers initiation of contact interaction with other souls on the journey there—to offer an example—should a soul be placed in a continuous replay of interaction with another soul—and during this contact the soul's buttons are pushed—so to describe it there—or the soul's trait is challenged into action or reaction—then a probable or possible option is displayed in either a positive action enabling the soul to choose a positive motivating response—or the soul can respond in a reactive, negative, or non-motivating of soul growth choice of doing the same thing as it has always done—for example—emotional crying or withdrawal—or returning the challenge—or analysing that the fault must be owned by itself—or the change of focus with distraction—will help them work it out as their emotions bubble up within their Team Body of Mind—Ego—and Soul—with a possible display of health harm to the Body.

If the action approach is taken when the buttons are pushed—or a challenge to the soul is perceived—then the option of choice remains open to action that supports the Team growth—and could include the walking away from the challenge—and exiting a relationship of repetitive challenge—merry-go-round-role-playing—or the action of reviewing all the soul's options—and taking stock of the situation—as you describe it there.

Another approach would be to recognize the plan that your soul pre-set—and asking for the reminder to be given by the soul for the team to hear and act upon. Also in both cases of action and reaction—the choice to ask your Angels for assistance and guiding insight to your choice of best approach—can then lift your observation of a display given in front of you—in a recall manner—or in an impromptu playhouse of a perfect scene rendition of the choice of best—given to observe in a creatively amazing ALL love approach to the self-preservation and combined self-motivation of the soul's growth choice.

The lift to gain this insight does propel a forward movement into a lift of self-worth—and self-pride—or an inner pat on the back for getting it—or jubilation for seeing the light of assistance from The Source of ALL.

It is clear to the vision of ALL love that is expressed here—your path is well lit—it is to this light and reflection that we guide and assist—the awareness of your traits—and the action and reaction—does offer you the empowerment tool to make a change or select an adjustment choice to a challenge attack of your traits—we are always in position to assist and do so when asked.

It is clear that the available insight given to you now—will assist in tying this all together—so we begin to share here the gains in soul growth application.

a. Soul Growth Application:

It is to the access and implementation of intention in varying degrees—that assists the soul's growth—as it is the selection of a better choice—or the best choice in the above situations to propel forward movement of soul growth—it is also gains in self-discovery that illuminate the ALL love—and display the intricate pre-planning taken on by each soul there—there is nothing left to chance on your journey—there is an approach of best to apply to every situation—it is with illumination on your path—that the journey turns into awareness—and then this awareness lifts into enjoyment and lightness to engage fully the predesigned and value gain of each itinerary entry.

b. An Enabling Trait Scenario:

On an Enabling Scenario we speak here—the choice to enable another Soul in relationships does access to the Soul the Shadow Path application to their lives—and engages the Swing Exchange Venture—this is displayed when the Soul takes on the role of an enabler to another Soul—thereby expressing the saying there—*you promote what you permit*—as it is clarity needed to engage action rather than reaction in all challenges there—there is clarity needed to the enabler to recognize the role-playing as well as the act in the play being staged—it is clarity that the momentum for adjustment and change or re-selection of choice of best is recognized.

When a soul enables another to remain in the challenge or reaction position—the consequences can lead to a permanence of role-playing—and a stalled movement—this is evident in most long-term abusive or dysfunctional relationships observed there—it is the soul's selection to make peace—*not rock the boat* as said there—and to continue the repetition of reaction with another reaction response—creating a continuous circle movement—and therefore a stall in soul growth—this is described as a Shadow Path or Swing Exchange Venture—depending on the degree of enabling and the relief taken at times during the soul's choice to walk this Shadow Path of another soul's chosen adventure of challenging choices.

When the Soul accepts the role-playing of enabling—this circle movement to another Soul in a relationship or friendship—then both souls perpetuate this stall on their paths.

It is again the gift of awareness that is offered within The ALL love and supported by the illumination of better to best choices—this encouraging access to movement and action choices in varying degrees—or in leaps to correction of forward movement on the individual or the combination of both souls' paths—should this movement into action occur—the shadow is lifted and the relationship or friendship is enabled to move into a supportive journey with a returned balance to both souls—and an encouragement recognized to engage the light of awareness.

In some cases there—when one soul in the relationship or friendship makes the choice to move into the choice of action—the second soul will engage also—mostly out of curiosity—observation to check out the display of newfound courage—or risk taking on the part of the first soul—and will choose to follow suit as not to be left behind—this is evident when the situation has assessed many years there of enabling.

However—should the choice be made on the part of the second soul not to engage the curiosity movement—then the Shadow Path no longer exists—and the previously enabling soul is freed to walk their own path with renewed lightness—to engage insight to their empowerment of self-motivation and self-preservation into forward movement.

In this case the independent soul will need or require a system to success—and prevent steps back into another Swing Exchange Venture—and setting up a new scenario of enabling—as the resonance of this reaction will remain within a memory of a negative comfort for some time there.

It is wise when the gain of illumination occurs—that the soul independent of enabling circular movement—does prepare an insight of action choices to implement and rehearse—to facilitate this change of choices in action—some suggested choices of action would include a renewed self-discovery of needs—wants—and wishes that focus on this singular soul—the lifting of a refreshing storyboard or trip tik mapping *(like a journey continuing with the flip of the page; or a list of dream wishes to project into the future.)* of the soul's future adventures—and also an engaging of new and reinforced scheduling of meditation guidance to open this soul's connection to The ALL Source and empowerment of ALL love awareness.

In the event of a mutual or joint decision to discontinue a Shadow Path—or temporary Swing Exchange Venture with both souls on the stalled movement role-play—a movement or action decision into awareness and illumination would also include a discovery of each soul's traits—talents—and abilities—would be recommended to offer a renewed understanding of each soul's wants—needs—and wishes—then the movement to the completion of this play and a mutual agreement to an accepted empowering descriptive roles of each to engage—with the new performance into a positive and rewarding relationship—which could result in accolades of an example of empowerment in relationship or friendship—and nomination for Academy Awards may be noted there—as mentioned prior the choirs of Angels would be singing here—and a heavenly celebration would be the presentation prescriptive.

Accessing the tool of awareness gifted to all souls on their journey there—does engage the vision to the big picture of The ALL love—and return the power to place the soul into the position of driver on the adventure chosen there.

As the Mind and Ego engage the wisdom of their Soul presence—the Team then begins to access the power of being Soul-driven forward into the joy and lightness of its predesigned itinerary and events played out with synchronistic delight and awesome clarity to choices of best. *(A divine source takes the lead when the Soul is recognized by its team energies of Mind, Ego and Body.)*

A Shadow or Secondary Path can then move into a Parallel Path expressing mutual gains

and rewarding friendships and relationships—a Swing Exchange Venture could then become only a temporary step off of a soul's intended path—with a quick return to the insight of original intent and individual movement—to excel forward movement and action of soul growth itinerary as pre-planned.

A reminder and refreshed energy does engage in both scenarios there when the recognition of reaction or action choices and applications of each is lifted into each soul's insight—and thereby engagement of The ALL love lightness within and without.

My Mind grasps:
This insightful information is flying in daily as this book is compiled. Wow! Amazing! These words continue to be my expression as I type it up. *You promote what you permit!* This has never before held such in-depth understanding. You are sure right with your comment that it continues to get more insightful. Do you have any further comments, Soul voice?

My Soul responds:
Well, yes, I will always comment. You are now grasping the intricate details that were pre-planned prior to my securing a safe place in our Body here. Emphasis on the maintenance of a balanced lifestyle with good nutritional health has settled in for the Team, so now we move forward to further illumination together. I remain always available to offer my knowing for choices of the best for positive Team action. More fun ahead!

c. Expression of Talents:

The Angels of The Light continue:
Here we continue—the awareness of traits then encourages the lightening up of gifted Talents—for example these may be in music or art—or can be in problem-solving—know-how adaptation to the task at hand—also with an insightful approach of best—or the gifts you were given in Talent to display vision-of-an-uniquely-new-approach to creative design—etcetera—a gifted talent comes in ease to the soul—and is accessed usually without thought to this ease of ability to access this talent.

The expression of Talent is coupled with Ability—also the environmental experience gained within the life there—the talent may show up early as in ability to speak several languages—or sit and play an instrument of music without training—the talent may also express itself later on the journey when the gains of experience and exposure are gathered to enable a coming together of the divine timing illumination to display the gifted talent—as in writings of gathered knowledge or wisdom of insight.

The talents are gifted to assist the soul's journey and can be shared with the Team—as in the expression of the Mind outward—or the attainment of the Body and Ego in athletics—the Soul does share these gifts to facilitate its forward movement into positive action—should these gifted talents be used to express negativity—the depletion or waning of the talent becomes obvious.

Expression of the talent is offered positively when shared with other souls on this adventure—for example—as in comedy to engage the healing energy that lifts the body.

The expression of the gifted talents from The ALL love does offer a further access to soul growth as a team effort into action—when engaged in the positive—the talents are shown as amazing abilities and gather the admiration of other souls—in an exemplary display—talents are gained in gifted display to the adventure taken on.

d. Layering Adventure (Adoption):

In the case of a loaded or Layered Adventure as in example—the agreement to birth and accepting the possibility of being raised by another soul or group of souls—as well as the predesigned awareness of probable adoption—when this possibility or probability is accessed there—the traits and abilities of the birth parents—plus the exposure of traits and talents of the souls engaged in raising the adopted Soul are doubled up—and this then indicates the Soul's path is a layered approach to soul growth.

This layered application is selected to gather a double scoop if you will—to the lessons and insights of the Earth School—in an attempt to succeed in a double dose of soul growth.

When this is the path taken—the Soul is likely to feel overwhelmed at points or junctures on the path—as they may not have access or ability to glean the traits and abilities of the parents of birth.

This is when a look to discover the somewhat hidden clues within the birth names and the adopted names can lift insight to the direction, purpose, and mission chosen by the Soul—and lead to an emphasized approach—these Souls are not unlucky with their itinerary plan—but rather have taken on the double-layered application to achievement focus.

Uncovering the hidden clues and gaining this clarity—does lift the overwhelming burden with the emphasis placed on the double mission chosen—rather than a feeling of separation or unknown beginnings—and can lead to amazing growth of their Soul in quick strides—this is a similar case when the Soul is placed in an environment that does not encourage soul growth—and release from that enclosed or hardship environment—facilitates a look back—to only retrieve the positive lessons and gains—to assist forward movement.

Again here we remind of the free will gifted to all souls—to access and express choices made whether these choices are positive action or a negative reaction—the choice will always remain yours—as a Soul of The ALL Source energy intention.

Section 13: Angel Alerts:

We move now to the Angel Alerts we offer to engage your attention on this Earth School—these Angel Alerts can include the use of your sense of sound—with doors slamming unexpectedly or lights going on and off for no apparent reason—we also present to you in the sound and vision senses of our words of guidance and our display of sight.

An Angel Alert can be a huge wakeup call to the soul or soul's team—of an intervention needed on the path—it can also be of divine timing to begin awareness to engaging the chosen mission in earnest at that point.

An Angel Alert is offered as an announcement of the time is right—to lift awareness—and it can include words of direction heard there on Earth School—or both worlds *(Heaven and Earth)* and a vision of attention getting proportions—the Angel Alert is the taking of The ALL love intention and placing it on display to alert your attention to what you are engaging in or what is suggested as your next best choice of application there.

The Angel Alert is offered in a way to access your attention—however never place you in a feeling of harm—it is always surrounded by the space of safety and peace with the awareness of time seeming to stand still for you there.

The desire is to present a shift of focus—or to present an attention to the focus of best to engage next.

The Angel Alert does offer insight—that guidance and the excitement of the seemingly unknown to you—it creates a milestone on your journey that appears to excel from that point—Angel Alerts are only given with the divine timing of the ALL love engaged and the need for this Angel Alert message apparent.

a. Lightness of Path:

It is in the move now we engage your awareness of the Lightness on your continued Path—the access to lightness is not to be taken lightly—yes—we do express humour here—the placement of forward movement is to lift into lightness and ease to facilitate soul growth—this lift is of an awareness gathered with insight gain of The All Source—to lift and engage this movement into Lightness.

As it is the emotion and expression of joy that is one focus example chosen to engage on the journey—it is the added movement lift into lightness that enables the impact or mark—as you say—that a soul can leave behind on this Earth School for the observation of others and example to application to their own paths. *(We can leave behind a notable mark or memory of our work of passion. A passionate love approach for the work does then display the necessary lightness to enable an impact and example on other souls of this Earth School.)*

This lightness is attained when the acceptance of The ALL love is engaged by the team of Mind—Ego—Body and resides with the Soul.

The journey is lifted into lightness of awareness of best choices and lightness of step placement to access forward soul growth—as the Soul's voice is heard clearly by the Team.

Lightness is a celebration—a rejoicing on the path—and a lifting of the veil of forgetfulness—as this action is undertaken—the lightness of the wishes of intent are given—an aura of colour to lead the Soul forward on the path of soul growth—with a clarity to The ALL love connection—and also Angel access of magnificent insight to the ALL awe of wonder presented on the Earth School—a lightness to observe with the colour of Angel assistance with each step of forward action.

It is of lightness the ALL Source does offer to all Souls taking this adventure of choice—and it is to this ALL lightness we do combine our energies of The ALL connection to celebrate on earth and in heaven. It is this lightness that encircles and lifts the Soul—as it is also enclosed in the Body to offer further guidance to the predesigned path and the next itinerary events.

A seeking to engage this lightness does gather the Soul's needs—wants—and wishes up in a bow—or to express here it is the ultimate of levels the Soul does seek.

b. Steps to Completion:

We continue here with the Steps to Completion on your journey there—this timing is also planned in detail within your itinerary as previously mentioned—this is also coincided with divine timing and the engagement of both The ALL love and the welcoming team of heavenly family.

It is the shared involvement of all concerned

that is called to attention when the soul's journey is completed—the preparations are made and the welcoming party set to engage.

If the Soul has taken—a just-in-time approach to embracing the ALL love—this Soul is also guaranteed a reception into the ALL love welcome—however the party is of a subdued nature in comparison—it is the example—of the last-minute-change-of-mind approach—that the door does open to accept this change—however—the preparation to a celebration has been kept on hold for this Soul—and the engagement to the display of party favours as mentioned previously—is held for display after the debriefing process has been successful—where the Soul embraces the ALL love in full measure.

The Soul who engages the ALL love with Joy—Lightness—and Intention—to positive action choices—whether full success has been the result or not—the welcome home is multiplied into an exuberant lifting of unique expression characteristic to the Soul's desires—and the celebration of this Soul's awareness of The ALL Source is awarded levels of soul growth recognition—we do enjoy the celebrations here in heaven—and also the preparations to this celebration—with the acknowledgment of positive choice intention to action expressed during the Earth School adventure.

c. No Judgment of The ALL Source:

We move now in the No Judgment of The ALL Source—with this we offer to you the illumination of a parent with full love to the child—the ALL Source does not judge the souls' journey—this may come as a surprise to many there—the ALL Source love is a protective and welcoming love—it is of no judgment or condemnation—it is of a full observational approach with judgment withheld—and in this way the Soul is encouraged to review their journey and Earth School adventure with guidance to the points on their predesigned itinerary—offered for comparison and observation to the level of soul growth attained—it is with this review of the journey taken—the intricate soul growth—that a keen attention to successful aspects of the journey are noted—these successful aspects of achievement are praised by the review board of the ALL Source team—and a move to delete the aspects that begin with a focused intention—but did not continue to a successful completion—these are erased of this review—yet noted to add to a future incarnation itinerary of the Soul's choosing—to again attempt.

This then confirms the message often given there to the Souls who journey on the Earth School—it is the intention—the attempt—and the approach to positive choice success—that is recorded as soul growth—the notations are clearly noted in detail to assist an improved approach of possibility or probability of success for a future incarnation of the Soul's choosing.

The erasing or editing of attempts that were not completed successfully is archived for future access—the Soul's focus intent—delivery approach—and choices of action and reaction are also noted—and the level attained is recorded as well—the uniqueness of each Soul's journey—is reviewed by the heavenly team—as well as the Soul—comparison to its predesigned itinerary—the detours—ventures—and full on approaches—are also noted—with every detail retained to assist the development of future itineraries—this journey on earth has been an intricate and challenging school of soul growth application.

The praise of success is noted by the Soul from the heavenly team—and with the encouragement to attempt a future incarnation at the Soul's ready junction and desire—the review is ended—noted—and archived to be referred to at any time the Soul desires.

What is next? Well an audience with The ALL love is the reward for taking on this Earth School adventure—this allows the Soul to express gratitude for the opportunity and gifts received to enhance success—as well as acknowledgment to the team of support from the Angels—Spirit Guides—Earth Team—and Heavenly Family.

When in this audience with the ALL Source—the Soul is enlightened to the need for these adventures of growth for the energy intention of the Source of ALL to accomplish the growth of these Soul energies into the insight of the ALL Love magnificence.

This is an opportunity to embrace this unconditional—total—and eternal love—to also fill up of this ALL energy and celebrate one's Soul energy existence—as a piece of the whole—this is undertaken as the expanse of the Soul's need for a recharge—to thereby engage in the celebration that awaits.

When the Soul leaves the audience of The ALL Source—it can choose the Souls present at the celebration—and—mentally you could say however—it is an energy projection that it recalls the ability to access—and thereby sends out these energy projection invitations to all heavenly entities of energy it wants to attend its party—no crying—no reviewing—no apologizing takes place at this party—the party is pure jubilation for the Soul's return home—and accolades for the growth achieved.

As you remember—there is no time frame here in heaven—so you could say this party goes on forever—and it does—after every incarnation this Soul chooses to apply to its Soul growth.

d. Debriefing Scenario:

It is now time to offer a Debriefing Scenario to all the souls there on the Earth School adventure—your approach in action or reaction is attained in awareness—this awareness is gained with an intention to seek insight—the insight is gained by the movement into positive focused growth—and the growth is achieved by the selection of choices to experience and lessons—learned and taken from each choice played out in self-motivation and self-preservation—with the attention maintained to balance Earth School Team of assistance—of the Mind—Ego—Body—and Soul.

The attainment to engage success is to listen and encourage your Soul voice—to engage your Mind with the Ego in participation on a positive note—and the teams noting to the nutritional needs of the Body—thus enabling the team's journey to the finish line—in the carriage of its desire and pre-design.

The assistance from The ALL is always available when asked to assist—in the form of Spirit Guides and Angels—the Angels also facilitate messages of familiar alert recognition of a predeceased loved one—and it is important to note here—this loved one does only have a small guiding yet important message to deliver to you—in an attempt to initiate a lift to see clearer your choice at that junction of your journey.

It is in the comfort of the heavens the loved one waits and prepares to welcome you home—and in the meantime of no time—the loved one does engage itself with further growth and selections of its own.

You are always accompanied there by your Team—as well as your Spirit Guide—and your Angels—as selected prior to incarnation—this ALL Love energy maintains their vigilance over you as you attempt this Soul growth journey—and returns with you here to heaven in all its glory.

You are truly blessed—do lift yourself to this insight—move yourself to the ease of joy and lightness on the journey there—with the knowing you are embraced and held safely tied to The ALL Source love and energies—as you remain a piece of The Whole.

As the adventures continue and the insight engages—your path is well lit ... The Angels of The Light.

My Mind speaks:
The Source of ALL assistance is truly never ending, and the assistance on my path of Soul growth deeply moves me. We send a hug heart felt team hug of gratitude to all these guiding Angels.

The Angels respond:
Thank you for the hug—we celebrate your growth and return Angel hugs back to you.

The Angels of The Light offer this reflection: It is of this poem following here—we do select for you the beacon of light to guide the thought and to embrace the flow—we are of The ALL love—we are of The ALL One—as are you—it is to this—the journey does turn and seek a bigger picture—it is of this journey you are directed—and it is of this journey you do seek to clearly see—we share this with you to open further your insight to the big picture—to see a vision of ALL One love—it is of this gain that the joy of the journey is encased with each step—and is open to investigate for clues—it is of the gain to lightness you do open to abundance to manifesting and to lifting into lightness the ALL connection—the seeking to see does motivate your movement and does engage for you the wonder of reflection in reflection—as the mirror image is reinforced and displayed—we are with you every step—embrace this thought—we walk together—we assist your insight—your reach to joy—your steps into lightness—the lift of this knowing is the empowerment you seek.

The Angels of The Light offer this poem:

> The guidance of mankind—
> the soul energies of The ALL—
> is of a continuous flow.
>
> The opening of awareness—
> does lift to engage—
> a seamless connection—
> a reinforced lightness—
> again to remember—the embrace of The All.
>
> This taking of adventure—
> with desire to growth—
> does capture the vision—
> and illuminate the oath.
>
> The return to ALL love—
> resides securely within—
> a beacon of guidance—
> to motivate and prompt.

**The blessings abundant—
the journey embrace—
a vision of ALL One—
to register in grace
... the Angels of The Light.**

**Your journey here—
is a journey of discovery.**

**The refection of a mirror—
does elevate—
assists in elevation—
to soul growth—
… The Angels of The Light.**

Chapter Thirteen:

Who's Cookie Are You?

Vision of Confirmation—Recognition Exercise—Five-Part Harmony —Emotional Awe —My Soul Song—Words from the ALL Source.

My Mind reflects:

During the process of receiving this book, I was consumed with curiosity of what title would become the perfect fit. To recognize when the Mind attempts to take the steering wheel on this Soul driven journey, is the challenge. Driving to a hair appointment one day, the phrase—*Like a flash in the pan!* —jumped immediately forward to grab my attention. Was it a summary comment to my mind's thoughts? I realized my Soul was present in this internalized conversation. With this recognition, I quickly concluded that this phrase could be a suggestion for the book title.

Did it fit? My life has seemed to flash by so quickly, when reviewing. I have discovered that there is a prompting or lead-in from my Soul to see the direction or reason for everything here on my journey. I must quietly listen to its wisdom and not go running off without verification.

During my appointment, I shared with Meredith, my hairdresser, that *A Flash in the Pan!* could be the title of the book I was writing. She quickly responded with her Piscean intuition, *This may not be the title you end up using, as there are many other possible titles out there.* Guidance comes in the most amazing way. Could her comment be guidance voiced through her from my Angels? I know that the Angels can offer guidance through others while accessing any of our six senses to alert us.

How has this work with the Angels changed me?

Over the years, I have become selective of whom to tell about my Angel work. The reaction of some people indicates that they think I am strange. Yet their reaction is often awkwardly strange themselves when in my presence. Some people who are secretly guarding an Angel experience of their own are elated to finally share their story without fear of judgment. I believe we all have an awesome story to share because Angels are with each of us and become very involved with guiding our life mission here. We need only to acknowledge their assistance.

Absorbing the insight from The Angels of The Light; acknowledging a team effort with Soul guidance; and grasping that ALL energies reside within me. This places a vision of the big picture of soul growth front and center. My desire to search for more insight seems to evolve with another awesome discovery. The choices of action initiated in ease, joy, and lightness excites and stirs in me anticipation. My team seatbelts are securely fastened and I am reassured in the knowing we have so many divine companions. *Acceptance that everything is as it should be! That all the intricate and divine reasons unfolding, guiding, and embracing my path are events of possibility or probability in my pre-designed itinerary. That I have only to ask for a glimpse and remain alert to messages of wise guidance.*

The angel-spirit-artist Toby, who divinely facilitates the Angel portraits in a presentation of visual messages that persists in pliable reflection for others here on this earth journey, puts me continuously in the emotions of awe. These channellings support my role as a messenger. In addition, I want to mention here my improved clarity to the assistance from Soul Entities residing in heaven. They offer divine clues of their presence via my Angels. *Thanks for the beautiful signs, Mom!* My future calls me onto a road becoming much more traveled.

Reviewing is still on my Mind:
I was still formulating how I would absorb all this insight and readily recall it. While reviewing my itinerary entries, the approach of a matter-of-fact presentation becomes obvious to me. These writings appear to be void of emotion. It reads like a manuscript of a play of life, with actor side notes to fill in the emotions and build the character, once the play is in action. A plan of approach surfaces; *place marker events like Swing Ventures* to my life review filing system to help digest this insight. This could then provide a categorized quick access review of the many choices I have experienced

and also alert me to future and imminent choice options.

Challenge appears to direct and excite the Soul when planning the itinerary I am told. It knows that a reserved position of observer after birth is the placement it occupies. Becoming fortified within our body, it often chooses to experience an abundance of insightful lessons for soul growth. It then offers up guidance as our own wise Soul voice prompting us. When in heaven, our Soul is void of emotion other than expansive everlasting love. It begins this journey to experience the lessons with emotions attached and is very present on this chosen schooling adventure.

A reminiscing of my lifted memories:
What could I possibly write about myself that would fill even one page? Any desire to hold onto this thought was dismissed as the Angels opened a floodgate of memories and observations of how life seems to fall into place. I have selected a few here.

Joy in all its essence lifts me into self-motivation and becomes a big part of my life mission. I have given weight to the concept that I chose my mother for the observation she could provide plus to have my soul experience her strength and talents. Also, I have tweaked this knowledge she offered, making it uniquely my own expression. From my father, I have mimicked his quiet, soft-spoken and slower demeanour and fine-tuned this approach into my personality and approach to life. I recognize that choosing to birth into the Messenger family gave me a great childhood with sibling fun plus surrounding myself with many cousins, not to mention the clues within my surname. This realization has filled me to embrace my Soul's chosen mission and *deliver this important message of celebrating Angel love.* A further insight is that I have been delivering messages of joy on a small scale all my life. I must have subconsciously liked the fit of *being a messenger.* Who knew?

The cookie story:
My mother told me a story from my childhood. The best part of this memory is her delight in telling the story. She became animated and also changed her voice to mimic me at approximately three years old.

I spotted a cookie on the floor under my baby sister's high chair. My mother was cleaning up after lunch and witnessed a cute conversation I had with a cookie. I balanced myself over the wooden rung of the high chair and began the conversation.

Are you Marilyn's cookie? My little voice would deepen, answering in my interpretation of the cookie's voice.

NO! I replied.
Are you Linda's cookie?
NO!
Are you Darlene's cookie?
NO! The cookie's voice was deep with conviction as I spoke for the cookie.
Are you Gloria's cookie?
YES! With that confirmation, I picked up the cookie and ate it.

Mom would then break out into laughter and tell me how she had to hold herself back from laughing aloud at the time. This is a precious memory I will forever cherish of connecting with her.

Four young daughters to present to the world:
My twin aunts tell me this story of how Mom placed a lot of her attention and energy on dressing and grooming her four little daughters. She would clean and polish our little white shoes every evening and then line the shoes in a row to dry overnight. This footwear had to be ready for active running the next day as we chased the chickens and played outdoors while visiting on my father's family farm. Another memory I recall is when we would take a short test drive on the big dump truck that my Dad was working on, as four little giggling girls and two adults would be tightly packed into the front bench seat and off we would go for a short visit with family on my mom's side. It must have been very crowded—no seatbelts back then. This adventurous, elevated view of our city would also include a lecture from Mom, to behave ourselves once we arrived. Discipline was the rule back then. Stress was evident too; it did not escape our family. For all her wonderful traits and talents, my mother was one to be reckoned with. She knew her mind and was not to be disagreed with. *Her greatest teaching was to always reach for what I wanted in life and hold on to the belief that I was worthy of what I wished for.*

My teaching of God and the Angels came from the United Protestant Church:
We conveniently lived across the street from the church, yet I do not remember Dad attending. Mom

taught Sunday school when her girls were young. I recall her dismissing my questions of - *Why would God be mean to us?* She did not encourage my inquisitiveness in this way. *Did her faith include a God who disciplines?*

Life renews in visions around me:
In my youth, I witness a devastating invasion of fuzzy caterpillars attacking the leaves of our small forest of birch trees in our front yard. This invasion of hungry insects covered the tree trunks as well as the ground. It was a gross and terrifying sight; the precious trees were stripped completely of their leaves. However, the next year, the trees were renewed to full splendour without a trace of devastation. Our front yard vision of a perceived tragedy gave to me an insight of how nature rises above stress and is renewed. *Most caterpillars turn into beautiful butterflies—do they not? An inspirational vision of preservation and renewal was displayed to take us through this life adventure.*

Listening skills:
I have an innocent memory of sitting on a huge truck tire in our driveway, holding my hairless doll and chatting away to my father, who was a class-A mechanic. Engaging my Dad in conversation was difficult as he was a man of few words. However, I was happy with the occasional grunt I received from him. Never telling me to go away and play elsewhere he made me feel accepted. His patient listening was an example to me to listen to others in my life, respecting their desire to voice an opinion. Recalling my childhood memories places me in a position of recognizing the lessons given

by my parents. Though my memories were not all great ones, this review lifts to me a glimpse of their attempts to be a perfect fit of parental guidance that I required to begin my soul growth team adventure on this predesigned itinerary.

A significant impact:
Viewing a big-screen production of *The Blue Planet* had a huge impact on me. It presented the breathtaking beauty of a seemingly fragile positioning of our world floating in the universe. The documentary was delivered through the lens of a camera located on a space station. It was a breathtaking sight! Talk about the big picture. This vision has been forever carved into my mind and serves as a reminder of the significance of our life journeys here.

Intuitive knowing:
A feeling that pushed me at times to make a decision quickly was a strong inner knowing that unstoppable change was on the way. My decision to quit my job and travel to Europe with my best girlfriend was not as much of a surprise to me as it was to others. Inner knowing guided me to believe in a positive outcome for all concerned would be the gain. It shows definite divine timing when a review is taken. *A Swing Venture* description fits this adventure to clear my emotions of the end of my first marriage and their resulting stall to my life. This adventure allowed me to observe a bigger picture. It helped me to become unstuck with what to do next in life. I believe the prompting from my inner companion began to again surface.

A vision of confirmation:

When my Mother passed on, it was four days before Christmas. My husband Bill and I were driving home Christmas Eve afternoon. Heavy snow clouds filled the horizon as we traveled south from this northern Canadian city. Deep in thought wondering whether Mom had happily reached heaven yet, I lifted my eyes to the horizon on the road ahead. I gasped in surprise of the vision in the sky. My husband chuckled and said, *I was wondering when you would see it up there!* For several minutes, this vision had held in this dark gray sky filled with overburdened snow clouds.

Wow! I exclaimed to this unbelievable visual delight. Displayed in front of us was a beautiful rainbow between the dark clouds. The clouds appeared to be cleanly sliced, spread open and acting as book ends to suspend this rainbow in the sky. *Oh, I see a similarity!* Some of these dark clouds near the rainbow transformed into white fluffy clouds as we watched in amazement. They resembled the fluffy whipped flour icing Mom used to pile high on our birthday cakes. Her special icing would fight with the birthday candles for our attention with its self-sustaining top curls. This memory tempted me to reach out and touch this seemingly reachable vision. Just wanted to poke my finger out the car window and flick into the clouds to have a taste test. *I was mesmerized!* We were staring with the hope of holding on to this breathtaking vision. The clouds came slowly together and completely hid this rainbow phenomenon after several minutes. *We agreed that it was a sign!* Mom was saying she had made it safely to heaven. She was putting her baking skills on display immediately after arriving. She must be smiling, making this huge statement and remarkable vision with help from the Angels. *Thanks, Mom, I now see you were also using heavenly party favours to give me this sign. (rainbows)*

Additional communication was received from her for some time after her passing. This communication was narrated by The Angels of The Light with Mom's comments thrown in. The automatic writings led me to believe that she was adjusting well—yet there were a few comments made by the Angels that she was challenging the debriefing sessions. That sounds like my mom. During most of her life, she maintained a strong belief in God and the Angels. Two years prior to her death, she shared her own Angel encounter story in my Angel Awareness newsletter.

Clues are everywhere:
The awesome realization of the hidden clues within my name surprised and delighted me. This led to a genealogy search into my family name and turned out to be a labour of love for me. The resulting book of the Messenger family was bound in a paper reminiscent of birch bark. How interesting that repetition lifts and engages my memory here of a renewal in nature observed in childhood! *Can this renewal be applied to our approaching reunion?* A profound scripted statement appears on the front cover - *In every conceivable manner—the family is the link to our past—bridge to our future.* A strong sign of family love confirmation and also synchronistic guidance in my search to find the

perfect cover for the Messenger family history and photo album book.

Synchronicities:

I am aware of many synchronicities in my life that are displayed beyond coincidence. One that comes to mind does engage and connect the expanse of distance with a display of small and huge miracles. During a call with my stepdaughter Nancy, her in Trinidad and me in Canada, she mentioned that a new inspiring saying had come to her attention. *If you always do what you have always done—you will always get what you always got!* To my genuine amazement, this very same saying had been printed on a bookmark that fell out of a book titled, *How to Organize your Life Inside and Out*. I had picked up and put down this organizing book three times before finally purchasing it at our second-hand book sale that was a fundraiser to offer support for the parents of a new miracle baby fighting for her life, my great niece. The saying had inspired me also when I read it. These synchronistic connections in life continue to amaze me! *They reinforce how intricate our journey is played out with the Divine timing of The ALL script that is facilitated by our Guardian Angels.* A successful book sale resulted and my great-niece made a miraculous recovery, which was the reward for all who participated.

Spiritual growth:

My spiritual growth has strengthened to the degree that motivates this open Mind team effort. The embracing of my team removes any thoughts of separation instantly. An ALL Oneness reinforced value of self-worth that includes my Body, Ego,

Mind, and Soul prevails. This gift of insight then expands my recognition of a team adventure. With my own uniquely predesigned spiritual journey being well lit by The Angels of The Light, in their role of messengers from the ALL Source, my future holds miracles. Discovery of the cleverly placed clues to empower recognition of this life adventure continue to surface. There is sure to be some heavenly sweet reward for this detective work once completing this Earth Schooling. *Possibly a heavenly cookie?* Until I receive this graduation reward, my intention remains strong to be part of *a team expressing our true values as Gloria's cookie!*

Entry: Itinerary glimpse from The Angels of The Light.
The book you write will be of much insight and encouragement of many other souls—as the Angel Awareness newsletter surprised and surpassed your concept of circulation—so will this book—you will be inspired to also prepare your coffee table book with the visual collection of Angel portraits and miracle stories to further celebrate your mission choice.

My Mind inquires:
Are we starting to move forward now in leaps and bounds, Soul? My numerology friend informs me that there is a rare planetary event taking place in Pisces causing radical changes in people's lives. Is this event assisting and fuelling the spurt of spiritual growth I am sensing. Are the Angels sharing energy of The ALL Source enhancing our paths with the colour of light? *Are my colours yellow and blue?* I

am noticing vibrancy of colour everywhere. Can you lend me your voice, Soul?

My Soul responds:
Your path is well lit and enhanced with the light colours of yellow and blue, yes. You are moving forward with intent now. Colours will begin to fit with your every choice selected there. Everything is aligning to assist this growth of insight to you, including the astrology signs. Are you holding on? We are on the fast track; it is going to get better!

My Mind engages:
More adventure! I will be listening. Do not want to miss anything. Please feel free to turn up the volume, Soul.

Entry: Itinerary glimpse from The Angels of The Light.
You will begin to see how every event in your life has been predesigned with your participation and involvement anticipated in action—to enable illumination of the message—when choosing to respond with a reaction approach—the mirror of revelation reflects your responsibility in perpetuating the continuous circle—and resulting return of the lesson to be presented by yet another scenario and group of Soul family participants—you now see there is a reason for everything—and insight offered with each choice made.

My Mind shares:
This guidance was offered to direct a release of the blocks that may hold back the team from a revealing reflection. The Angels offer this simplistic

Who's Cookie Are You?

yet powerful exercise when applied. My instruction was to make a list of all the people in my life who have in some way impacted my destiny or pushed on my emotional buttons of hurt, fear, anger, and regret by their actions or comments directed to me. Then make columns *(three or more)* and head these columns with the person having the most history in my life.

For example: Mom, Dad, Sibling, or Spouse names heading up each team column and representing the uniquely different lessons offered.

Make each column generous in size to allow for a written note by each name. Then place in the columns all the other people you have listed. Each person will indicate a fit in the individual columns when comparing similarity in personality traits to the head person of the column.

Once all the people on your list have found a home in the columns, the insight expands. Beside each name write how you have responded to the hurt, fear, anger or regret emotion that was experienced. Write a word beside each name. Choose your response note from only two words: *reaction or action*. For example, did you choose the response of a reaction approach that continues the replay of manipulation/pressure or stress? Did you choose to stand true to yourself and take on the consequential fallout to enable your self-preservation in a choice of action? This will offer recognition of the choice of action or reaction made in each encounter and therefore offer forward guidance to see a bigger picture of overall encounters with each column of lesson-bringers.

This exercise is not to attach blame; it is to

recognize our choice of response to participate in each lesson brought to our attention. A return to empowerment is the gain from this exercise with the rebalancing of our ALL energies within the ALL Love. A bigger picture offers clarity to our part of responsibility and involvement within each lesson or event in this predesigned adventure. A quick tally of the two words of choices—*either action or reaction*—can be very insightful.

The final step of this exercise is to genuinely engage The ALL love and release. Mentally thank these individuals as they may have played their role perfectly or not. They may have unwittingly pushed you forward in your life. However it is history. Now to release this summary of negative experiences, place them all inside an enormous bubble of water. This visual of a huge water bubble holds all the negative history you have had with these people. The water bubble is lifting into the sky and gaining exposure to atmospheric pressure. You now witness an explosion of confetti droplets. A healing, a releasing, a cleansing of blocked emotions are now tiny drops suspended on the wind and disappearing into the expansive space of the universal. We have lightened our journey to embrace a positive action choice. We can now move forward with renewed awareness.

The Angels of The Light encourage:
As the grasp of insight within this exercise is recognized—the advancement of your Soul growth is measured and celebrated in the Heavens with choirs of Angels singing applause of accomplishment to recognition—as we cheer you on with every step forward

into insight there—you are truly blessed and held safely within The ALL Love.

We say it is to the enlightenment gain of the situation you can use a change of approach—we suggest less control—as in allowing the thought that there is a reason for everything—when feeling controlled the reaction choice to get even becomes an off-balance pattern—a new approach of ease—is to ask for understanding and this choice does not give the raise of reaction to take as a personal affront—in most instances the event is only a reaction of others—a venting and less of an attempt to derail you—it is only their way and approach chosen to their own release—it is this you take a moment to observe—that this person is responding to the position of feeling jockeyed or pushed around by others.

It is a need here to recognize the severity of repetition of reaction choices—gain clarity of the lesson—in the mirror reflection. *(Ask self, could I have reacted like this before? What was my self-positioning and involvement to my prior reaction? Take a moment to observe self in the mirror and what justification for our emotional reaction was projected. Then choose action.)* **Move into the emotion of compassion to engage a softer way to bring forgiveness to the surface and prevent your emotional swing.**

As this approach does not work on all situations—it is a full-on action with the softening of the raw emotion that can be repeated and does lead to forgiveness.

This adjustment of release does take on a journey and a creation of trust in self to engage the path in clarity—a trust of gifted abilities and movement into lightness and joy.

This is of a looking glass journey started and to continue—the Soul knows the itinerary plan—the growth desired—it desires to be lifted and healed to the point of full lightness and joy—the healing is noted as the effects of emotions harboured and carried as baggage—the Soul is on this Earth School to experience emotions and jog through to experience a return to full insight and to engage in this awareness—of the mirror vision of ALL love—yes—the Soul does also agree to forget and regain some of this insight to enable the exercise to continue and to blend the insight with action on your path in assistance to others—yes—it is a double focus to remember for self and to assist others—your Soul has lifted and is ready to move forward to assist others.

This book will open the door for others and your team to forward gains—you as the Mind do also engage the mirror effect with the desire to mimic the Soul and these desires—it is of this your Ego and Body also take up this focus—your energies of Mind—Body—Ego—and Soul do come together and move as one—up to the heavens when the journey is complete on this Earth School—yes—you the Mind—you the Ego—and you the Body do merge of energy—and the case or form does return to dust—this is in another mirror effect to observe—as it is of a gain here to express the need for an approach of unison—to reach the completion of this Soul growth insight—yes—there is further growth desires for the Soul—yes there is a joy and lightness that is sought—it is to this level that you engage in the freedom to express self and journey onward—to engage the full insight of the mirror—when we say the Mind and Ego are twins—we say they are of the same energy and degree of energies—they are to recognize each other to work effectively for the team—they are part of the intelligence of the Soul energies—as is the Body with its automatic function of routine—it is also part of this Soul energy intelligence—we do present this mirror image to you—gain the awareness of the team—it is in this the empowerment begins—your team is made up of Soul with this energy of the Soul reflected into the Mind—the Ego and the Body—you are ALL One as a team—and the mirror extends this thought to be ALL One with the vision of your team being part of The ALL One with the ALL Source.

My Mind opens to this insight:
Empowered to engage this insight is my Mind's conscious thought as I begin a morning check list with my team.

- ❖ **My morning check list of a Five-Part Harmony Team!**

A Mirroring Discovery with Angel Visitation—Gloria Messenger

Check list at the start of my day:

- **Mind—stay open to the wise guidance available to our team... √**
- **Ego—my twin, only thoughts that empower the team recognition... √**
- **Soul voice—I invite you to speak up loudly throughout the day ... √**
- **Body voice* - direct my attention to healthy nutritional choices ... √**
- **Guardian Angels and Spirit Guides— the vibrations plus the energies of this abundant ALL Love—please alert me accessing our link-up signs ... √**

Check √ check √ check √ check √ check √ ... all in place now team, we're good to go!

* Understanding that my Body can receive a voice, by selecting an Angel that I can assign and name to speak for it sends me into selecting a name. Tallulah, welcome to the team! Your name jumped into my head and I love pronouncing it. My intention is now focused to attain and maintain healthier food choices in a lighter approach of ease. Health in balanced harmony is my goal.

Never Alone Again!
Alone is a word that appeared to fit me when I felt different from others in my life. Now I realize the true meaning as AL-L ONE. A total all-encompassing Al-one love that moves my team forward past the fears of separation with a passion to engage this journey that I believe will continue to clear into remembering. *If we lifted our mind to recognize the mirror of a heaven everywhere on earth, how would it engage our sense of awe? Do we already receive glimpses of what we already know to be true?* My Soul voice responds with a loud YES!

The Angels of The Light close this book with this insight:
From the mountains—to the valleys—to the oceans far and wide—God/The ALL does bless and offer this vision in heaven to duplicate on earth—a vision of ALL is needed now—it is of this the energies flow—yes—whatever your vision setting to be—that is the vision—it is to this we engage the mirror reflection—the look of ALL is of a need to express and to assist these in school there—*(Souls)* it is to this the need for this message—it is to this the purpose for the school—it is beyond the vision magnificence that we engage you - it is to this we seek to work further—a vision of ALL love.

It is of a full seeking that you do engage—it is of this that the journey continues—the placing of ALL within every aspect of life there—the placing of ALL in the turn to engage and to seek self—it is to the work of such that a seeking for clarity is given the mirror vision of The ALL Love—The ALL Energies in everything—everywhere—always present—always available and—always engaging.

Yes—it is this ALL vision that does lift and open you to the expanse of the reach and the expanse of the touch—it is in this that we do engage and to this we do work openly with you—the movement into joy and lightness expands your thought and growth—we do empty all the areas of doubt and reinforce the vision—we are of joy and we are of love—we are of ALL—as are you—as is everyone there.

We are of a seeking to see and a working to enable—we are of a journey to select and an

expression to engage—it is to this the work continues.

My Soul offers this refection:
The work of engaging here this full vision of ALL love does then open the ability to grow. It offers the ability to stretch and embrace the magnificence of the vision. A glimpse to sustain and also engage discovery to the mirror reflection is presented to lift into the knowing of The Source of ALL. We are together on this path team, and make great leaps with the application of this insight.

My Mind expresses:
My own channelled Angel portrait that I received seventeen years ago has evolved over the years, showing visual changes for my observation. It would appear to fade, then brighten, and then offer more Angel faces within the colours and white spaces. *Recently three large letters are evident and span the width of the portrait frame.* These letters seemingly lift off the portrait and this was not previously noted. *The letters are J-O-Y.* As this change has only surfaced to my observation this year, I believe it is an indication or acknowledgement of my intent and desire to reach this same level of joy and enlightenment. Feeling the Angels energy vibrations with me allows a smile to spread from the inside out.

The Angels of The Light offer:
We are in the vision of ALL and do open to you (*the Mind, Ego, Body, Soul = Team*) **this thought— it is in the expression—that we can only do what we can do—that the hold is there—we can reach many avenues of success when there**

is no limit put to the attempt—it is in genuine open release that we are to engage and to release the full-on approach—the journey of loving each step with engaging self *(the Team)* **in the release of same energies— to turn the energy of accomplishment up high—**

We are of ALL Source ability and to this we do express— the best choice will be presented to success of the big picture—the clues are of an ALL love approach and an open lifted optimism to enable the application of self-worth and self-knowing to lift up to engage your path of best.

My Mind is in gratitude:
The Angels predicted to me that this book would appear to come full circle and the title would be written upon completion. These pages of insight just flew in each day for just over a month. The writings lifted and expanded my thoughts. My gratitude also goes out to Ever-All-One, an Angel of The Light who facilitated the layout of conversational writings within this book.

Entry: Itinerary glimpse from The Angels of the Light:
The magic within these portraits continue to impress and engage the vision of growth— as these levels of movement are lifted to the recipient of the portrait—to enable the engagement of this growth acceptance—a magical journey with the emotion of awe— lifted to engage each reflective recognition of soul growth for you.

Emotional Awe!

I am in heightened emotion of awe again! It was suggested to me by several author friends, to come up with a temporary book cover in preparation to promote this book in advance to its printing. I requested my creative friend, Carolyn to search the computer photo galleries for a temporary book cover that would closely represent the title of this book. She wrote down the title and agreed to do this research when she had the time. To my surprise, the very next day I receive an e-mail saying - *Could not remove this task from my mind and awakened through the night with a compelling feeling to go to my computer. Then the first photo gallery site I opened displayed a mirror-image abstract photo attached here. This could represent the title well. Hope you like it.*

When I opened up her attachment, I could have fallen off my chair in amazement. *It was a remarkable resemblance of the very first Angel portrait received!* This was the portrait of my husband's Angel channelled seventeen years prior. It definitely is a surreal likeness of his Angel portrait, he confirmed. We noted a change only in the colours and that this photo gallery image appeared as a zoomed-in close-up of his portrait. *Carolyn had never seen this first portrait! I believe she was guided to fulfill the intentions of The Angels of The Light to make this book appear to come full circle for me.* What an amazing circle completion!

A continuous emotional awe embraces me in the magic of this work I do with these Angels! They have my reflective colours of blue and yellow displayed within this heavenly synchronized book image. Then for further impact the interpretation of this book cover image was offered by the Angels—***A vision of ALL love—this is the ALL love—the gain to see in every blade of grass and in every vision of the universe—it is to this we reach beyond this vision.***

I believe this book cover has an important message for everyone. My desire for a temporary book cover has now embraced a permanent status. I invite you to interpret your own message with the interpretation from The Angels.

My Mind continues:

This amazing event and visual presentation lifts further insight. This book cover also resembles for me a close up photo of the head and eyes of a bumblebee. *Am I to be more aware of the small miracles of these tiny messengers?* The gain of these thoughts of insight secures, expands and engages my belief of the somewhat magical assistance offered on this Earth School. Wonder what is next to rediscover? As you know Soul, I am seeing it! Wow, the reflection can be presented in everything!

My Soul responds:

Yes, *the reflection is within the reflection and of the reflection*. The Angels can facilitate the use of all earthly energies to deliver a message, including a tiny insect. Once you begin to see these guiding examples with this life here my Mind friend, our team will advance to a secure level of lightness and joy. Keep open our channel of connection. I am preparing my song for your thoughts and ears.

Entry: Itinerary glimpse from The Angels of The Light.
The ALL Source does lift your team to see and engage the lightness and joy of this level of growth while on this Earth School—you begin to recognize the vision of your carriage—this does lift a joy and self-acceptance to the level of lightness you now seek—your team does begin to harmonize.

My Mind reflects:
I will anxiously wait to hear your song, Soul. Will expect to be placed in the emotion of awe again. In the meantime, I will revise my list of twenty descriptive items to describe my future work with the Angels of The Light. This will enable an open door between us Soul, with your prompts to dream bigger for life here. Now I have my five-part harmony team in place to take action choices. The ease of positive movement forward is the spot light application to engage and maintain.

My Soul replies:
As the Soul portion of this team, I would like to add this thought for our All-One future. The predesigned itinerary is displayed throughout our lives in reflection to engage our recognition. It appears in everything, and is seemingly everywhere, as it reflects what is unique to each of us. The journey of self-discovery can lift this personal itinerary to the Mind and Ego with a display to the smallest detail of our uniquely chosen mission. The clues become so obvious when discovered with the reward of insight to the gain of team Soul growth. Continue

to stay open to our illuminated future, my Mind companion.

The Angels of The Light announce:
We are of ALL Love and of ALL knowing vibrations and do offer you this song of your Soul.

My Soul begins to sing and my Mind reflects:
As I received this channelled song from my Soul, it is amazingly heard within my Mind and yet also simultaneously harmonizing in my ear.

A loving memory of my childhood sing-songs is lifted. *You are My Sunshine!* — I hear a remarkable similarity to this melody. A song repeatedly sung in unison with my sisters in our youth and also performed now at opportune times.

However, now I hear new lyrics! My energy is being transported to a joyful Omni /all-one space as I intently listen. Then guided to reflect upon the incredible synchronicity of my Soul team leader's musical selection! *WOW!*

❖ ***TO LIFT THE VEIL OF FORGETFULNESS!*** —*song from my Soul:* (© *lyrics*)

> The completion of — this first big step
> into light of ALL love.
> Our movement to see clearer.
> To lift the veil of forgetfulness.
>
> A journey we engage together.
> We are of this All team.
> We are given to ALL reflection.

A Mirroring Discovery with Angel Visitation—Gloria Messenger

The path again to seek and see.

(chorus) **The completion of
— this first big step
into light of ALL love.
Our movement to see clearer.
To lift the veil of forgetfulness.**

**The colour — of joy.
The path we seek remains with light.
Illumination of the open vision.
Truth reflected to embrace.**

(chorus) **The completion of
— this first big step
into light of ALL love.
Our movement to see clearer.
To lift the veil of forgetfulness.**

**Of this we do express our team
to the growth gain.
We are of this ALL love.
This continuous vision flow engage.**

(chorus) **The completion of
— this first big step
into light of ALL love.
Our movement to see clearer.
To lift the veil of forgetfulness.**

**A selection to display a turn.
To seek only when desire is met.
To seek again the brighter path.
We reach the level of ALL insight.**

(chorus) **The completion of
— this first big step
into light of ALL love.
Our movement to see clearer.
To lift the veil of forgetfulness.

The path of best the gain of awareness.
It is of each step we take.
Together awareness is offered.
Then we can choose to accept.

(chorus) The completion of
— this first big step
into light of ALL love.
Our movement to see clearer.
To lift the veil of forgetfulness.

The vision of a reflective love.
A love of ALL everlasting joy.
To this vision we embrace together.
And all enjoy the journey taken on.

(chorus) The completion of
— this first big step
into light of ALL love.
Our movement to see clearer.
To lift the veil of forgetfulness.

The work that does lift in ease.
To our grasp — our desire for adventure.
Discovery of insight.
We do open to design our own path.**

(chorus) **The completion of
— this first big step
into light of ALL love.
Our movement to see clearer.
To lift the veil of forgetfulness.**

**The choice of carriage the desire for growth.
We reach the success of this vision.
An ALL love of infinite embrace.
You hear my song — the music of my Soul.**

(chorus) **The completion of
— this first big step
into light of ALL love.
Our movement to see clearer.
To lift the veil of forgetfulness.**

My Mind discovers:
The song—*You are my Sunshine*—remains in dispute as to the musical and lyrical composer, however it is considered to be the most perfect song ever written and the third most popular song in the world, right after *Happy Birthday* and *White Christmas.* Now I am completely in the space of AWE!

My Soul offers further:
Allow this song to fill our body, our twins Ego and Mind, to repeat in a poem of love, a poem of joyful expression and in the sound of thought engaged to lift awareness of the Source of ALL. Allow it to filter through and engage our being as we do bond as one and embrace this path together. It is

of a celebration we begin here, and a celebration we return too. Let the seeking be of this vision to engage each step forward we take together. We are blessed, we are held within and of The ALL Love. We have success of mission within our reflective steps to this mirroring discovery.

My Mind continues to be amazed:
The hearing of your song, Soul, engages my senses and places me in a place of unity and peace with the amazement of the ALL love. A reflection back to childhood and the seeing of your colour of sunshine, my Soul companion, brings this insight to a total acceptance. It is a truly loving embrace to our team as we take this life adventure of further all-one discovery here!

The Angels of The Light write:
We are to say here—the journey is always well lit and the turning to see in the half-circle motion—is the observation of formulating a plan—and seeking to engage the wisdom of ALL Love into this plan.

Entry: Itinerary glimpse from The Angels of The Light:
You are surprised by the full-on and open acceptance received to this book—*A Mirroring Discovery—with Angel Visitation* when it is launched—you seek to move further into sharing the messages you received and you are now in total acceptance of your predesigned mission journey—as you indulge in this thought—reach to enable this vision to be placed securely in your Mind—Ego—Body—and Soul—to engage in the open vision of

success—with this vision in place you do open to The ALL abundance—The ALL love—The ALL energies of observation on the mirror journey of discovery—you have undertaken with intricate attention to detail on the path of choices—you are of this ALL love—and within this ALL love to seek and rediscover this connection—this sustaining of energies—and this open engaging—engage and observe the mirror reflection offered to assist you in every choice of best—your Angels of The Light.

❖ **Words from The ALL Source:**

A Journey of the Return to Oneness!

It is of a combination as of The One.

It is in a look of the Whole in overview.

It is of a look of the connection within.

The turn to engage the choice of best.

The turn to embrace the seeking to be.

The knowing of self—
the look within—
as it is the connection.

It is of a choice always and
of a timing to select—
and grow to the awareness of self—

and the connection of self
to the ALL Source—
as it is in this knowing the answers
you seek become clearer.

It is in the look to self—
the look to a grand plan—
the look to free will—
the look to the choice of journey there.

It is to the overview of this
selection—you see.

You see the turn to a view in making—
a view in taking—
a view in assistance—
a view in embrace of The ALL.

It is in an open visual knowing
that the journey is set—
and adjusted and set—
and adjusted.

It is in this The ALL love does
embrace and lead—
as it is a reflection of The ALL you seek.

The reflection of self.
The reflection of self of oneness.

As it is taken within—it is
expressed without.

A Mirroring Discovery with Angel Visitation—Gloria Messenger

It is in a view—
the view of ALL—that the
recognition of self does occur.

It is to this we do expand and assist—
with the guidance offered
and the love engaged.

It is within and without the balance occurs.

It is in the selection—
the choice of self-discovery
of the Oneness—
that the reflection does engage.

The reflection of The ALL
is within each soul–
and thereby the soul is self-directed to
the selection of the journey of discovery.

The journey of return to Oneness.

It is in this the magnetic pull—
the turn of all energies.

It is in the seeking—the seeing is engaged—
the growth does occur.

It is in this you are truly blessed—
and held in The ALL abundance—
of eternal—total—and unconditional love –
... The ALL Source.

Conclusion

As writings in this book can open thought to endless questions, a concept of summarizing the heavenly insight appears insurmountable yet practical and necessary to me. I offer here my comprehension of these insights received via The Angels of The Light and via The Source of ALL.

The major concept offers a knowing that we *(our Soul team energies)* are solely responsible for the pre-design and initiation of our itinerary intentions here on earth. We journey here as an energy team of Mind, Ego, Body, and Soul. We are never alone on this path and should we desire to reach to the Divine guidance of assistance offered, our paths become reflective with illumination.

With a life review, I can recognize many choices accessed by me, including swing ventures. More in sync with my carriage than ever before, I have delegated a permanent seating arrangement with my Soul in the driver's seat. Our carriage I understand is the expression of our inner character, traits, talents, abilities, and personality displayed proudly in our own unique approach. The self-discovery of this illuminated reflection is very empowering. Who is pulling my carriage? This revelation will forever place a smile on my face as it represents my passion to see life clearer. This is again a mirror-reflected within the characteristics of my long-time favourite childhood animal of the wild kingdom. The neck of the giraffe allows me to observe the near future and to cover ground quickly to embrace my joy of change. A perfect symbolic character reflection of my own unique approach on this journey.

The concept of a Heaven on Earth being a mirror

refection of guidance does lift one to challenge that concept. Yet, I have had moments when a glimpse of a still space, amazing beauty, and the miracle of birth and re-birth confirm this thought. These and other awesome moments literally have taken my breath away. There is no room in my life for doubt.

I believe the magic within these Angel portraits channelled through me display change that reflects movement in our lives and illuminates our level of growth. Ever-changing is a word of two-part-reflection that must truly represent our lives and our world.

JOY-PEACE-TRUST, these passions motivate our journey and our choices. It is my clarity now that when upset or in a reactive state of being off-balance, I can take my own emotional pulse.

A Mirroring Discovery with Angel Visitation! - is the name given for this book by The Angels of the Light. The descriptive content of this Earth School of discovery is offered to ignite the passion with mystery still compelling further discovery within us.

I am encouraged to ask the Angels for clarity at every step, as this trip is engaged with lessons of guidance. It is a truly remarkable *Journey of a Return to Oneness!*

As a messenger delivers an important
message, I deliver this question to you.
Are you ready to open to your Angels?

Glossary

* *Funk & Wagnall's standard desk dictionary (revised edition)*
** *quoted from The Angels of The Light.*

** Angel Awareness ... is the rebirthing of your knowing and the observation of the seemingly invisible.

** Angel Hugs ... a request from The Angels of The Light to embrace you, at any time or any place, as it is a seemingly invisible embrace of love felt.

Aura * ... an energy field of colour surrounding the human body. A distinctive air or quality enveloping or characterizing a person or thing in light.

Automatic writing *... to offer, direct or convey through an open channel. A relaxed meditative or quieting the mind resulting in receipt of written messages of insight, poems, and wisdom from a higher source.

Ego * ... part of the conscious mind. The thinking, feeling, and acting self—that is conscious of itself and aware of its distinction from the object of its thought and perceptions. The ego fights for control of self by reinforcing separateness and often pushes with inner dialogue to do things out of character or obligingly instead of with delight.

** Ego ... the Ego is a twin voice with the Mind in unison; a motivator and preserver.

** Emotional pulse ... the awareness gained, and recognized when the rhythm of life moves into clarity of balance or off-balance. This then offers choice to unravel the puzzle of reaction choices.

Six senses * ... the six faculties or receptors the human body uses continuously during regular daily functions. These consist of sight, hearing, smell, taste, touch, and intuition.

Soul * ... the rational, emotional, and volitional faculties in man, conceived of as forming an entity distinct from the body. The divine principle of life in man. The disembodied spirit of one upon death.

** Soul ... the soul is colour energy of The ALL Source contained within the human form. The soul pre-designs its uniquely individual itinerary events that are selected to move its team energies of Mind, Ego and Body in a forward momentum of soul growth achievement during this earth school adventure.

Synchronicity * ... the awe and meaning that lifts the thoughts beyond the coincidence of an event and into the wonder of the workings of the universe.

Endorsements

A Mirroring Discovery—with Angel Visitation! This amazing book needs to be read by ALL who believe in the influence of Angels in their lives and ALL who still doubt. You will definitely see things more clearly and be able to look at the world more through the eyes of our friends in high places!—Carolyn Shannon, *What Really Really Bugs Me Sometimes*

Finally! Courageous, insightful, and thought-provoking. Gloria's book, *A Mirroring Discovery—with Angel Visitation!* has answers to the every present question ... Why? Well done!
—Terri McCallum, Broker with ROYAL LePAGE Realty.

Reading this captivating book has tremendously heightened my spiritual awareness. One feels a releasing of old patterns while absorbing each chapter! The Angel messages within Gloria Messenger's personal story have now started me on a deeper spiritual journey. I encourage everyone who wants to grow to the next level to read this empowering book. Gloria Messenger and *A Mirroring Discovery* will change your life forever!
—Sue London, *Soar Above It ALL*